DISCOVERING THE EDEN VALLEY

DISCOVERING THE EDEN VALLEY

HIDDEN PLACES, CURIOSITIES AND STRANGE EVENTS

CHARLIE EMETT

WITH PHOTOGRAPHS BY RON DODSWORTH

SUTTON PUBLISHING

First published in the United Kingdom in 2005 by
Sutton Publishing Limited · Phoenix Mill
Thrupp · Stroud · Gloucestershire · GL5 2BU

British Library Cataloguing in Publication Data
A catalogue record for this book is available from the British Library.

ISBN 0-7509-4184-7

Typeset in 11/13.5pt Janson.
Typesetting and origination by
Sutton Publishing Limited.
Printed and bound in England by
J.H. Haynes & Co. Ltd, Sparkford.

Contents

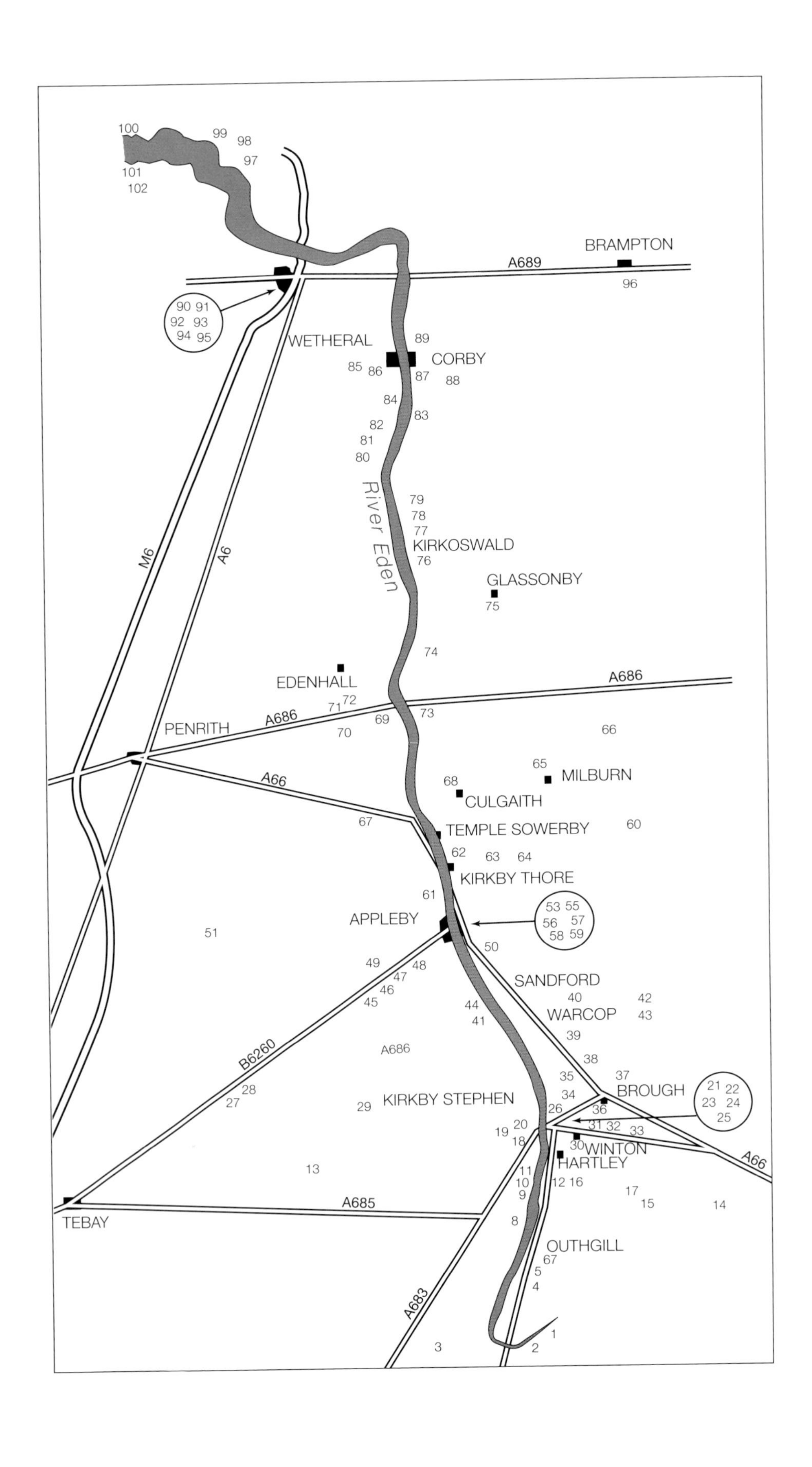
BRAMPTON
A689
WETHERAL
CORBY
River Eden
KIRKOSWALD
GLASSONBY
M6
A6
EDENHALL
A686
PENRITH
A66
MILBURN
CULGAITH
TEMPLE SOWERBY
KIRKBY THORE
APPLEBY
SANDFORD
WARCOP
B6260
KIRKBY STEPHEN
BROUGH
WINTON
HARTLEY
TEBAY
A685
OUTHGILL
A683

KEY TO MAP OF THE EDEN VALLEY

1

OS Grid
Ref: 786985

This is number 1 of the ten Eden benchmark scultpures (see page 32). Situated on Lady Anne's Way, Mallerstang, *Water Cut*, by Mary Bourne is made of salterwath limestone.

INTRODUCTION

For James Hilton it was Shangri-La, and for Dorothy 'somewhere over the rainbow'. But my piece of heaven on earth is in Cumbria, in the Eden Valley, which lies between Lakeland's eastern fells and the fells of Shap to westwards, the Howgills to the south and the High Pennines to the east It is a vale of great beauty, watered by Cumbria's principal river, the Eden, which the Romans called Ituna. The river rises on Black Fell Moss, near Hugh's seat, 2,260ft above sea level, beginning life as headstrong Hell Gill Beck. Nurtured by several feeders, this fast-flowing beck soon enters confining Hell Gill, exiting as the River Eden, celebrating its transition almost at once by plunging over Hell Gill Force, the highest waterfall along the river's length. The youthful Eden descends wild Mallerstang, the 'morass of the wild duck' spilling over spectacular cataracts and gliding across smooth dubs, swiftly losing height.

The Eden leaves Mallerstang in slow fashion, along a brockram bed, pitted with pot holes, one as wide as the river itself. The brockram ends abruptly at a deep pool which marks the southern most limit of the Eden Valley's sandstone bedrock. From this dark dub the whole of the Eden Valley is predominantly sandstone. So for most of its life the River Eden meanders through rich, fertile countryside where, here and there, red cliffs rise sheer from clear water.

The Eden Valley abounds in strong, historical associations. The Romans and, later, the Normans built a string of forts and castles along it to deter would-be aggressors. Subsequently, the valley suffered Scottish invasions and the English armies arrived, intent on punishing the Scots. All the castles and churches destroyed by the Scots were, much later, restored by a most remarkable person, Lady Anne Clifford, Countess of Pembroke.

Lady Anne is in good company. Uther Pendragon of Arthurian legend lived in the Eden Valley, at Pendragon Castle, as did Sir Hugh de Morville, one of the three knights who killed Thomas Becket, Archbishop of Canterbury, on 29 December 1170. Sir Andrew de Harcla's seat was Harcla (Hartley) Castle. Sir Andrew was the only Englishman respected by Robert Bruce. Then there were the

Howards, the Musgraves and the Whartons, all exalted Eden Valley families, who played important roles in English history. The illustrious Mounseys are descended from Armand de Monceau, who lived during the reign of Edward II. In 1745 the Mounseys settled in Carlisle and played a major part in establishing Carlisle's calico business. In 1808 William Henry Mounsey, the great Cumbrian eccentric, was born. Through his efforts the bond between Gentile and Jew has become stronger. The Revd George Bramwell Evens, 'Romany of the BBC', fell in love with the Eden Valley and settled there. He introduced many city children to the joys of nature through his *Out with Romany* programmes. He was a great communicator who brilliantly conveyed his involvement with and love of the Eden Valley to entranced listeners every week. There are many more people like these, whose links with the Eden Valley are strong. All have led remarkable lives, influenced in no small measure by the beautiful Eden Valley.

The 100 points of interest selected here cover the full length of the Eden Valley, from the top of Mallerstang to the Solway Firth; and are presented in two parts, upper and lower Eden Valley. Three interrelated maps – one of the whole of the Eden Valley, one of the Upper and one of the Lower Valleys – show where each point of interest lies in relation to the others and to towns and villages; and each point of interest has a grid reference, so you should have no difficulty getting there. Leaving may be a problem, for such is the attraction of each point of interest that tearing yourself away may prove difficult.

Chapter 1

The Upper Eden Valley

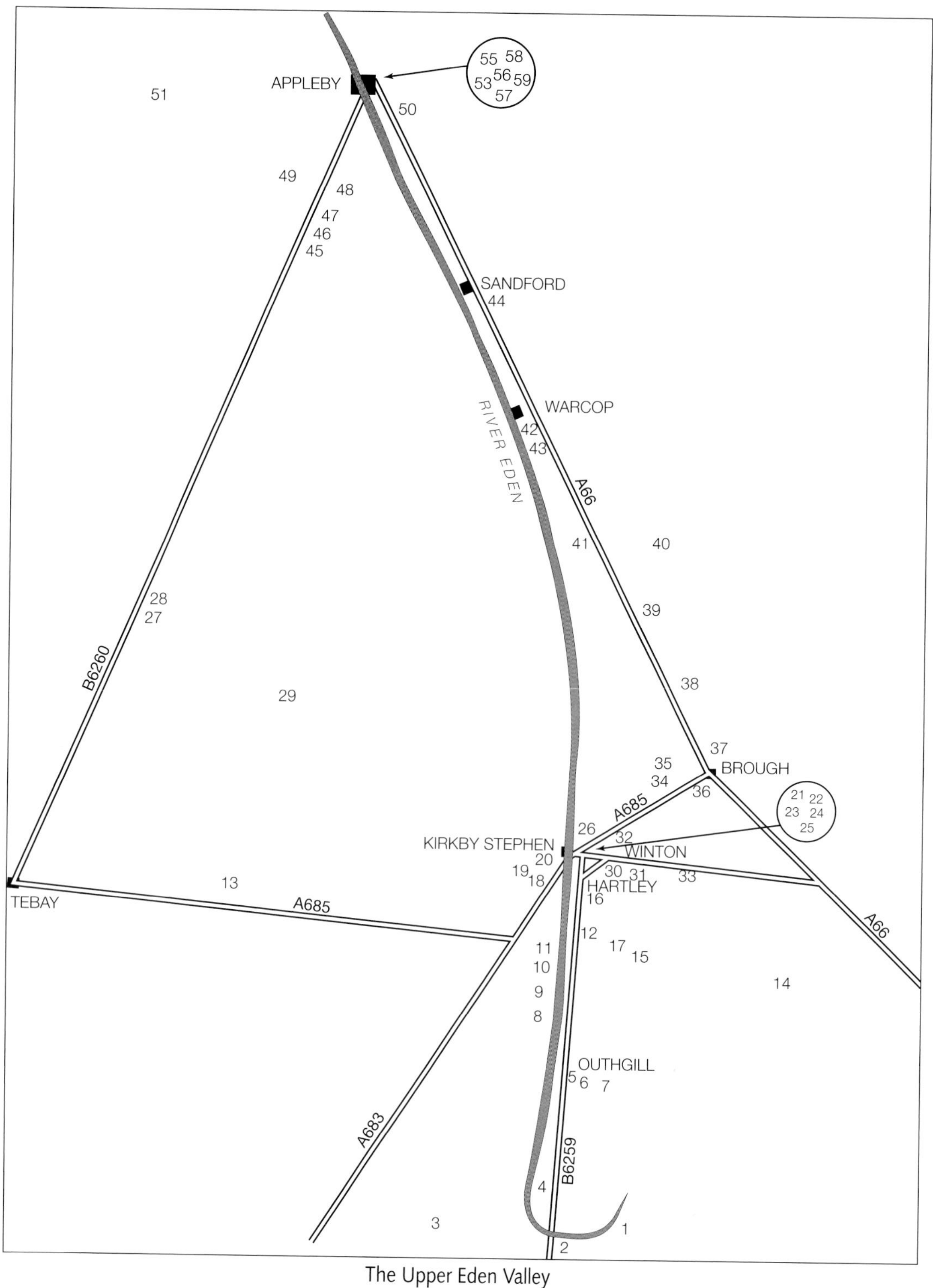

The Upper Eden Valley

HELL GILL BRIDGE

Angram Common, at the head of Mallerstang

2
OS Grid
Ref: 785969

Hell Gill Bridge crosses a gorge through which the infant Eden flows before it plunges over Hellgill Foss, the river's most spectacular waterfall. The rocky gorge, in parts 90ft deep, is so narrow at the top that an active person with nerves of steel can jump it. But the obvious and only sensible way across the gorge is on Devil's Bridge. At one time the only road through Mallerstang crossed Devil's Bridge and every autumn a continuous procession of drovers, farmers and dealers with their horses, cattle and sheep used the road, Lady Anne's Way, on their way to Brough Hill Fair. Many locals with an eye to business set up stalls at Devil's Bridge for the sale of refreshments to these travellers.

3
OS Grid
Ref: 758988

WILD BOAR FELL

The Head of Mallerstang

Wild Boar Fell, a triangular wedge of high ground that dominates the head of the Eden Valley, is a true mountain. Made of sandstone and capped with millstone grit, it is perched on a limestone plateau. From the Nab, a column precariously positioned on the escarpment's highest point, magnificent all-round views embrace the Howgills, many Lakeland mountains, Cross Fell, Ingleborough and Wernside. An Ordnance Survey column, 2,324ft above sea level, marks the summit of Wild Boar Fell, which is so named because legend has it that the last wild boar in Westmorland was killed there by Sir Richard de Musgrave. Sir Richard died in 1442 and was assigned an altar tomb in the Musgrove chapel in Kirkby Stephen parish church. When the tomb was removed in about 1847 a boar's tusk was found in it, thus supporting the legend.

LADY ANNE'S WAY

North-east from the Thrang, Mallerstang, to Shaw Paddock

4
OS Grid Ref: Northern end: 783004. Southern end: 786952

Now a rough track that climbs north-easterly from the B6258 near the Thrang to Shaw Paddock, Lady Anne's Way was once the only road through Mallerstang. It kept to the higher ground to avoid the marshes lower down, crossing several water splashes and bridging the Eden at Hell Gill gorge. Every autumn, enterprising locals selling refreshments greeted travellers moving north to Brough Hill Fair, driving sheep and cattle, were met at Hell Grill bridge, where Lady Anne's Way crosses the Eden. When the Midland Railway Company opened the Settle–Carlisle line in 1876 the importance of Lady Anne's Way declined.

5
OS Grid
Ref: 781015

SAINT MARY'S CHURCH, OUTHGILL

Outhgill village, Mallerstang

Idonea de Leyburne is believed to have founded St Mary's Church in about 1311, although the bell is thirteenth century. The incumbents' stipend was made up solely of contributions from local farmers. As early as the eighth century the clergy all over Europe had the right to the tenth part of all the produce of church lands and livestock and these tithes were paid to the parish priest. In Mallerstang, all land was absolutely free from payment of tithes of corn and grain but tithes were paid on hay and agistment. St Mary's Church had no burial ground until 1813. A headstone in the churchyard refers to a dentist 'filling his last cavity'.

MICHAEL FARADAY, 1791–1869

Outhgill, Mallerstang

6
OS Grid
Ref: 782015

James Faraday, a native of Swaledale, was for many years a blacksmith at Outhgill in Mallerstang. He married Margaret Hastewell, a servant at Deep Gill Farm, also from Mallerstang. They moved to London, where their son, Michael, was born in 1791. Following a very elementary education, Michael was apprenticed to a bookseller. This enabled him to read any scientific books available, especially those on electricity. He had an enquiring mind and after much study he eventually became the greatest of all physical philosophers in Europe. He discovered benzene and the laws of electrolysis, invented the dynamo transformer and the electric motor. Faraday Gill, in Mallerstang is named after him, and Kirkby Stephen's one-time Beck Lane is now Faraday Road.

7
OS Grid
Ref: 783016

THE JEW STONE

Outhgill Village Mallerstang

On 15 March 1850 William Mounsey walked the full length of the Eden and erected a monument, the Jew Stone, near the river's source to commemorate his achievement. Sigils and texts in Greek and Latin were carved into the monument along with the Star of David. The Jew Stone measured 7ft by 7¼in by 3in. In 1870 the Jew Stone was vandalised. During the Second World War Shalom Hermon, a Polish army officer based at Catterick, saw Jew Stone on a map and became interested. Further investigations convinced him that the Jew Stone had strong Jewish connections. Long and complete detective work followed during which the author and Stuart Dean retraced Monsey's walk to raise funds towards a replacement, which was erected on Outhgill village green. At the unveiling ceremony Shalom Hermon, now Minister for Sport and Culture in the Israeli Government, asked, 'Is it mere chance that "Shalom", meaning "peace" in Hebrew and "Emett", meaning "truth", have come together to bring about this important link?'

PENDRAGON CASTLE

8
OS Grid Ref: 783026

B6259 Half a mile north of Outhgill

Uther Pendragon built Pendragon Castle in the mists of time alongside the River Eden to defend Mallerstang, 'morass of the wild duck'. He tried to moat it by altering the course of the Eden, but failed, as this couplet relates:

> Let Uther Pendragon do what he can,
> Eden will run where Eden ran.

After passing to the Vipont and Clifford families, Pendragon Castle was strengthened in about 1300 by Robert de Clifford. In 1341 the Scots destroyed much of it by fire. Roger Clifford restored it between 1360 and 1370. Two hundred years later the Scots again set it on fire, and it laid in ruins until Lady Anne Clifford restored it. When she died in 1685 the castle was dismantled by the 6th Earl of Thanet, to whom Lady Anne's estates passed after her death. What remains is now preserved by English Heritage.

9
OS Grid
Ref: 772048

LAMMERSIDE CASTLE

Between Pendragon Castle and Wharton Hall, Mallerstang

Lammerside Castle, a fortified pele tower, is set back from the left bank of the Eden, midway between Pendragon Castle and Wharton Hall. It was built in the thirteenth century to guard the southern approach to the fertile Eden Valley. The name is probably a corruption of 'Lambert's Seat'; Pennant in his *Tour From Downing to Alston* refers to 'a very ancient, square building called Lammerside Hall, formerly (known) by the sad name of the 'Dolerous Tower'. At one time it belonged to the Warcop family. It is reputed to have been the earliest known residence of the Whartons or de Quertons before they moved to Wharton Hall.

WHARTON HALL

Between Nateby, and Pendragon Castle, Mallerstang

10
OS Grid
Ref: 772062

Occupying a high bank overlooking the River Eden downstream of Lammerside Castle, Wharton Hall is built around a courtyard and was once surrounded by a deer park. In 1540 a great hall with a large kitchen was added by Thomas, Lord Wharton. The gatehouse was added in 1559, and traces of the portcullis can still be seen. A tablet, dated 1559 and carved with the Wharton arms and motto 'Pleasur in acts d'armys', is sited above an archway marking the entrance to the courtyard. When, in 1617, James I visited Wharton Hall, Philip, 3rd Baron Wharton got so heavily into debt that he was obliged to set aside half his income to repay his creditors. In 1725 Philip Wharton supported the Jacobite cause and fought against his country in the siege of Gibraltar in 1727. For this act he was outlawed and his estates were confiscated. So ended the great house of Wharton after 500 years.

11
OS Grid
Ref: 771063

'LILI BOLERO'

Wharton Hall, south of Kirkby Stpehen

As a child, Thomas, the 5th Baron Wharton of Wharton Hall, the eldest son of Philip, a strict Covenanter, had an extremely disciplined upbringing, which included having to listen to sermons three hours long. When he came of age he rebelled by becoming deeply involved in the gaieties of London, a hedonistic lifestyle he thoroughly enjoyed. In 1715 he was created Marquis of Wharton. His main claim to fame is that he wrote the words to the popular tune 'Lili Bolero', which was said to have whistled a king out of three kingdoms. The song was adopted by the Commandos as their own and the BBC used it to introduce Forces programmes and news bulletins.

PREHISTORIC VILLAGE SETTLEMENT

12
OS Grid
Ref: 77048

East of B6259 1 mile south of Nateby Mallerstang

About ½ mile south-south-east of Thringill, a farm on the eastern side of the B6259, itself ½ mile south of Nateby, a rectangular enclosure of about 2 acres holds the remains of a prehistoric village settlement. Some 50yd south of the enclosure are the very faint remains of a circular hut 15ft in diameter. A bank runs east from the northern side of the enclosure as far as a wall, the field boundary. This is all that remains of an ancient British settlement. Nearby are several very well defined strip-lynchetts or cultivation terraces, with more a little further away, sure sign that the bottom of Mallerstang was populated by prehistoric man.

13
OS Grid
Ref: 726069

SMARDALE VIADUCT

Between Crosby Garret Fell and Smardale Fell

The now defunct branch line from Kirkby Stephen to Tebay ran along the rim of beautifully wooded Smardale Gill, high above Scandal Beck, which it crossed at the head of the gill on Smardale viaduct. Designed by the well-known engineer Crossley, the viaduct was begun in 1870 and completed in 1875. Unlike most viaducts, where the central spans are the deepest, Smardale viaduct's deepest spans are close to its eastern end, because of the lay of the land – the ground below the viaduct is deep clay, so the viaduct's foundations had to be sunk about 40ft before firm, red shale was reached. Dozens of sheep's fleeces were then placed on the foundations for added stability before building began. Smardale viaduct spans Scandal Beck at a height of 130ft, is a little more than 700ft long and its twelve arches are each 45ft wide. More than 60,000 tons of stone were used in its construction.

THE NINE STANDARDS

14
OS Grid
Ref: 828067

Hartley Fell, 3 miles south-east of Kirkby Stephen

Nine closely spaced stone pillars, all in a row, dominate the high fell horizon south-east of Kirkby Stephen. They are on Nine Standards Rigg, the southern end of which is crossed by the meandering Cumbria–Yorkshire border. At 2,162ft above sea level, the Nine Standards mark the northern end of the rigg and stand half a mile north of the county boundary: they are not boundary markers. The origin of the Nine Standards is wrapped in mystery. One theory is that they were erected to delude an enemy approaching from the east into thinking that people ahead were waiting to do battle; but this is fanciful. A more likely explanation is that shepherds built the Nine Standards to pass time. The Nine Standards are unique, and do not bear any relation to any other distinctive features.

15
OS Grid
Ref: 788073

THE TROUGHS

1 mile south-east of Kirkby Stephen

Having followed a fairly level course for about ½ mile Ladthwaite Beck spills over spectacular cataracts near Ewebank Scar. At this point a limestone outcrop edges Ladthwaite Beck. Many years ago a deep trench was cut through this outcrop at right angles to Ladthwaite Beck to divert water to Hartley. A wooden walkway was built along this trench just above the water level and the diversion was called 'the troughs'. From the north end of the outcrop the diverted water crosses the corner of High Out Wood, continuing across raised ground before descending to Hartley, flowing, if you can believe your eyes, uphill.

HARTLEY CASTLE

16
OS Grid Ref: 784081

Hartley Castle, overlooking Hartley Village, near Kirkby Stephen

Hartley Castle, near Kirkby Stephen, was home to Sir Andrew de Harcla, the only Englishman praised by Robert Bruce following the Scottish victory at Bannockburn in 1314. It was the ancient seat of the de Harclas, who had lived there since the Norman Conquest. Sir Andrew de Harcla rose to become the Earl of Carlisle, at that time the highest title of the nobility. Following Bannockburn, Sir Andrew became the only man able to check Robert Bruce's border raids. In 1322 Sir Andrew quelled a dangerous rebellion by defeating the Earl of Lancaster at Boroughbridge. The following year Edward II ordered Sir Andrew to negotiate peace terms with Robert Bruce, which he did, following long discussions. Meanwhile jealous courtiers discredited Sir Andrew to the king, who ordered Sir Andrew's execution. This was an unjust end to a great patriot who devoted his life to king and country.

17
OS Grid
Ref: 785073

EWEBANK SCAR

Ewebank Scar, alongside Ladthwaite Beck

The River Eden makes a most spectacular approach to Kirkby Stephen. It squeezes through a narrow gorge along a fissured bedrock of pink brockram to plunge into a large pool, Black Dub, edged with trees. The brockram ends abruptly at Black Dub, which is the uppermost end of the red sandstone across which the Eden flows all the way to the Solway Firth. Throughout the length of the Eden Valley this red sandstone is confined to the valley bottom, the valley sides comprising other rocks.

The awesome power of nature is shown in a most dramatic way at Ewebank Scar, almost a mile south of Hartley, where thousands of years ago a local fracture appeared in the carboniferous limestone of the Askrigg Block forming the eastern side of the Eden Valley. Orgogenisis, the intense vertical movement of the earth's crust along this fracture, caused its northern side to thrust upwards to form a very high, vertical cliff. About 700 years ago a guest called Ewebank staying at Hartley Castle chased a deer across unfamiliar countryside. It was a misty day with very limited visibility. The terrified deer, desperate to escape, leaped from the highest point of the limestone cliff. Ewebank's mount sped after the deer and also leaped over the cliff. All three were killed. The spectacular cliff is called Ewebank Scar in memory of the Hartley Castle guest who lost his life there all those years ago.

18
OS Grid
Ref: 775079

STENKRITH

The south end of Kirkby Stephen

On approaching Kirkby Stephen, the Eden funnels along a narrow gorge overhung with birch and rowan. Its bed is a pink, igneous rock, brockram, pockmarked with fissures and potholes, fashioned by countless floods. The parkland through which the Eden cascades so spectacularly is called Stenkrith, and is divided into 'High' and 'Low' by a bridge, beneath which is a pothole so vast it touches both sides of the river. This pothole, called 'Cowkarney Hole' by the locals, is dangerous because of sucking undercurrents. The noise generated by these undercurrents is known as 'the devil grinding mustard'. The main stream remains above ground to bewitch all who visit this enchanted spot.

19
OS Grid
Ref: 775075

EDEN BENCHMARKS

Stenkrith is at the south end of Kirkby Stephen

This sculpture collection, commissioned by East Cumbria Countryside Project to form a link between the rural and urban aspects of the Eden Valley, comprises ten carvings by different artists. Placed along public footpaths running the length of the Eden, the carvings also function as seats – hence their name, Eden benchmarks. They all have fanciful names. The one sited at Stenkrith, Kirkby Stephen, has angered most Kirkby Stephenites, including the author, because of its insensitivity. Stenkrith's bedrock is brockram, a conglomerate peculiar to Kirkby Stephen. Yet the sculpture placed there, called 'The Gap', came from hundreds of miles away and, at best, is out of place.

THE EDEN VALLEY LINE

Between Kirkby Stephen and Clifton

20
OS Grid Ref: Eastern end: 770076. Western end: 537262

The Eden Valley Line was 22 miles long and ran between Kirkby Stephen East station and Clifton Moor junction. It was opened on Saturday 7 June 1862, the trains stopping at all intermediate stations. Free seats were offered to anyone who cared to venture on the journey. The line linked up with two others: on the west, the Lancaster and Carlisle, which ran through Clifton and was opened for traffic on 15 December 1846; and on the east, the South Durham and Lancaster Union, which passed through Kirkby Stephen and was opened on 7 August 1861. The latter was linked with the Lancaster and Carlisle at Tebay.

21
OS Grid
Ref: 775085

KIRKBY STEPHEN'S CLOISTERS

North side of Kirkby Stephen market place

Sited along the north side of the market square, Kirkby Stephen's ancient cloisters stand at the main entrance to the parish church. For many years the cloisters have been used as a butter market on market days. Until the early years of the Second World War, when they were removed and melted down, splendid railings graced the cloisters: they have never been replaced. Custom decrees that the cloisters are locked at weddings until money is thrown to the onlookers, usually by the best man, allowing the newlyweds to leave the churchyard.

THE 'TRUPSTONE'

Kirkby Stephen's parish churchyard

22
OS Grid
Ref: 775085

There is a large, flat topped tomb in Kirkby Stephen churchyard that is reputed to have belonged to the Wharton family. Older than the Wharton tombs inside the church, it is known as the 'trupstone', and for generations money in lieu of tithes of hay was regularly paid on it to the incumbent on Easter Monday. This curious custom dates back to the reign of King Henry VIII or earlier. It was briefly put in jeopardy during the first decade of the nineteenth century when the Revd T.P. Williamson became vicar and refused to accept money paid in this way. But the parishioners contined to attend on Easter Monday as usual, and to tender their doles as before. When Mr Williamson died in 1835 the custom ceased.

23
OS Grid
Ref: 775085

KIRKBY STEPHEN PARISH CHURCH

Kirkby Stephen

Kirkby Stephen parish church, which dominates the northern end of the town, is the most beautiful church in the Carlisle diocese. Built on the site of a Saxon church, it dates from the twelfth century, although its 73ft tower was built in about 1500 to replace an earlier one that had fallen into disrepair. It has a glorious peal of eight bells and a custom of ringing curfew and taggy bells every evening at 8 o'clock, which dates back to the time of William the Conqueror. The church has side chapels dedicated to the Wharton and Musgrave families and some fascinating relics. One is a stone coffin which contained a female chieftain. When it was excavated in the mid-twentieth century, dozens of skeletons, not in coffins, were also discovered – probably evidence of massacre or plague. Another is a Saxon stone on which is carved Loki, the devil, in chains. The church is dedicated to St Stephen.

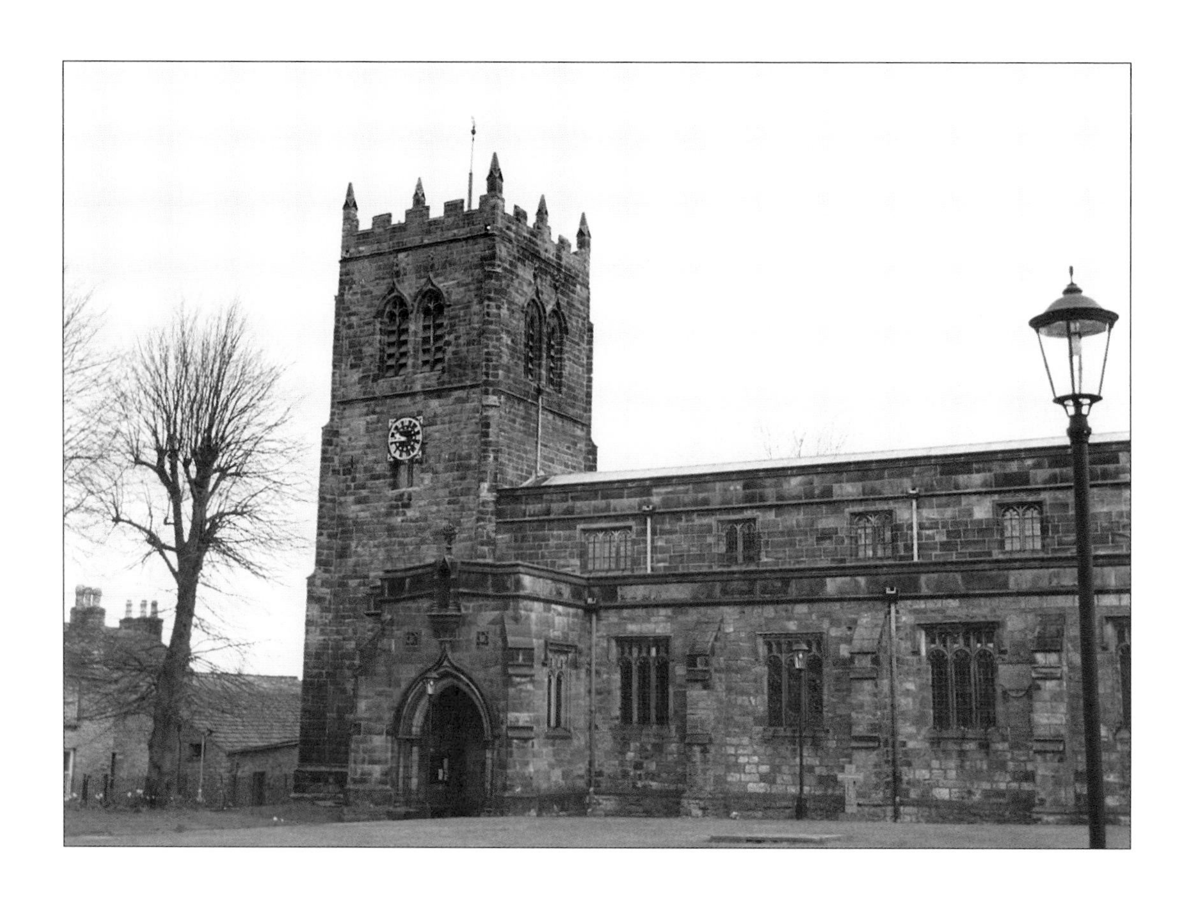

THE WHARTON TOMB, KIRKBY STEPHEN CHURCH

24
OS Grid Ref: 0775085

The Wharton Tomb, Kirkby Stephen Church

The Wharton tomb contains the remains of Thomas Wharton (1495–1568), the first of the family to gain a title. His tomb, with those of his two wives, has a Latin inscription which,translated reads:

I, Thomas Wharton, here do lie
With my two wives beside me,
Ellen, the first, and Ann, the next,
In Hymen's hands who tried me.
O Earth resume thy flesh and bones
Which back to thee are given,
An Thou, O God, receive our souls,
To live with Thee in Heaven.

The crest of the Wharton arms, a bull's head, is under Thomas's head. At one time this symbolised the devil in a vanquished posture. For this reason the inscription was paraphrased by a wag as follows:

Here I Thomas Wharton, do lie
With Lucifer under my head;
And Nelly, my wife, hard by
And Nancy as cold as lead.
Oh! How can I speak without dread?
Who could my sad fortune abide
With one devil under my head
And another laid close on each side.

25
OS Grid
Ref: 775086

HARTLEY CHAPEL, KIRKBY STEPHEN PARISH CHURCH

Kirkby Stephen parish church

Hartley Chapel on the south side of the chancel in Kirkby Stephen parish church is named after Sir Andrew de Harcla, 1st Earl of Carlisle (1260–1323) of Hartley Castle. A brass plaque in Hartley Chapel marks where he was buried by his sister. The Musgraves, whose tombs are also in Hartley Chapel, succeeded him. In 1847, during restoration work, a boar's tusk was found in Sir Richard Musgrave's tomb. It is thought to have belonged to the last wild boar killed on Wild Boar Fell. The chapel's roof bosses and parts of the screen are medieval and the heraldic shields are those of the Musgraves. The bushel wheat measure left of the altar belonged to the Earl of Thanet and was used to bring his tithes of wheat into the church.

'EDEN JAYS'

26
OS Grid
Ref: 776098

Eden Place is sited to the north of Kirkby Stephen

When Kirkby Stephen folk speak of 'Eden Jays' they are making a jocular reference to the parrots, macaws and cockatiels frequently seen in free flight around the town. These exotic birds live in huge bird boxes attached to some of the tall beech trees fronting Eden Place, a beautiful manor house. The owner of these multi-coloured birds ensures that they are well cared for and in no way restricted. There is also an indoor aviary where sick birds are restored to full health. None of these parrot species would survive a year in the Eden Valley without the food and care provided at Eden Place. They are all birds that forage more successfully in winter because then there are more fruits and berries for them to eat. Although free, these exotic birds always return to Eden Place, where they are assured of all the food and care they need, thanks to its beneficent owner who has made all this possible.

27
OS Grid
Ref: 685074

RAYSEAT PIKE

2 miles north-west of Newbiggin

Half a mile south of Sunbiggin Tarn there is a long barrow or burial mound 179ft long and on average some 50ft wide. It was built between 2500 and 2000 BC, the Neolithic period. When it was excavated in 1875 many large limestone and sandstone stones were found, arranged to form a trench with flues to maintain a draught while corpses were being cremated. During the excavation seven cremated bodies were found, and ox, horse, goat, sheep, pig and grouse bones scattered throughout the mound.

SUNBIGGIN TARN

28
OS Grid
Ref: 675077

Ravenstonedale Moor

Sunbiggin Tarn is most pleasantly situated in a hollow between Orton Scar and Crosby Garrett Fell. It is home to many different species of wild duck, coot, moorhen and snipe, while grouse are plentiful in the surrounding moorland. But this beautiful little tarn is best known as a gullery of black-headed gulls. Curiously, despite the fact that the black-headed gull is so common at Sunbiggin Tarn many people do not recognise it because its winter plumage does not sport a dark head. Within the tarn itself there are also several species of trout, some of which are quite large. But it is the sight and sound of the birds, in particular the black-headed gulls, that add greatly to the appeal of this enchanted spot.

29
OS Grid
Ref: 730096

CROSBY GARRET CHURCH

Church Hill, Crosby Garret

Crosby Garret church occupies a defensive position some 200ft above the village dominating the surrounding countryside. Parish historian J.W. Nicholson records that 'when beacon fires were burning in the north, Crosby and Soulby people gathered their stock into folds, the able-bodied men assembled on Stockber Hill to await eventualities. If danger threatened, there was the church to shelter those left behind.' Another legend tells that the church should have been built at the foot of the hill. But at night Satan carried the stones to the top, thinking that the old and infirm could not climb to the services and so would become easy prey for him.

WINTON'S BOARDING ACADEMY

30
OS Grid
Ref: 785106

Winton

Winton Hall, a three-storey Elizabethan-style manor house, now a farm, was formerly a 'boarding academy', similar to that at Bowes, County Durham, which was the original 'Dotheboys Hall' described in *Nicholas Nickleby* and in which Charles Dickens exposed the horrendous conditions prevailing in such establishments in the mid-nineteenth century. An advertisement in *The Times* of 22 June 1815, under 'Education', describes Winton Hall as a place 'where boys are educated, furnished with books, boarded and clothed by the Rev. J. Armathwaite, D.D. beneficial curate of Badley, at 22 guineas a year and parlour boarders at 40 guineas. There are no vacations at this school.'

31
OS Grid
Ref: 785106

WINTON'S FAMOUS SONS

Winton

Winton's most distinguished scholar, John Langhorn, was born in the town in 1735, just across the road from Winton Hall. He was a writer of great renown and his poetry influenced Robert Burns. Richard Burn, LLD (1720–85) wrote several law books and is best remembered for his *History of the Antiquities of Cumberland and Westmorland*, which he wrote in conjunction with Joseph Nicholson. Perhaps best remembered of Winton's sons were three generations of Thomas Pattinson, known locally as old Tom, middle Tom and young Tom. They were celebrated eighteenth-century clockmakers, who specialised in grandfather clocks that looked good and were excellent timekeepers.

KABER RIGG

Eastern side of Kaber village 2 miles north-east of Kirkby Stephen

32
OS Grid Ref: 799115

East of Kaber village there is a large common called Kaber Rigg, the site of the Kaber Rigg plot in the mid-seventeenth century. Following the Restoration, the Cavalier parliament passed a series of penal measures against nonconformists. One was the Five Mile Act, which caused insurrection throughout the country. Sir Philip Musgrave, a staunch Cavalier and principal supporter of the government in Westmorland, was, at that time, Governor of Carlisle. Captain Thomas Atkinson, the local leader of the Insurrectionists, arranged a meeting of rebels in October 1663, where arrangements were made to meet on Kaber Rigg with the intention of capturing Sir Philip Musgrave. A large number of Captain Atkinson's supporters failed to turn up, so the plot failed and Atkinson was imprisoned, first in Appleby Castle, then in London. He was returned to Appleby, where he was executed on 1 September 1664. That very day a courier staying in a hostelry on Stainmore exclaimed, 'Why! I have his reprieve in my pocket.'

33
OS Grid Ref:
839104

BELAH VIADUCT

East of Barrow station

At Kirkby Stephen on 25 August 1857 the Duke of Cleveland cut the first sod of a railway line that would cross the Pennines through the Stainmore Gap to connect the north-east ports to those of the Irish Sea. The engineer in charge of the project was a Scot, Thomas Bouch, and his resident engineer a fellow Scot, A.L. Nimmo. Bouch was later knighted for his work on the ill-fated Tay Bridge.

The largest of the few viaducts on this line over Stainmore crossed a broad, steep-sided ghyll through which the River Belah flowed. This was the Belah Viaduct, 1,040ft long and 196ft high – the highest viaduct in England and just one foot shorter than Crumlin Viaduct in South Wales, which was the highest in Britain.

Construction was speedy and comparatively uneventful. The navvies, however, upset the locals by their constant poaching. The Chief Constable of Cumberland and Westmorland offered to provide four policemen, but the railway directors would only agree to pay for one at a guinea a week plus 1*s* 6*d* boot allowance and one shilling for oil. Compared to this the navvies were paid 3*s* 1*d* to 3*s* 4*d* daily.

The piers of Belah Viaduct each had six 1ft diameter columns set in parallel rows of three. These were strengthened by cross-bracing every 5ft. There were also horizontal and diagonal tie-bars. The viaduct was 50ft wide at its base, narrowing to slightly less than half that at the top, which carried wrought iron girders on which the track was placed. There were sixteen spans.

Henry Pease of Darlington laid the foundation stone on 25 November 1857. The building of the viaduct took only forty-three days, a remarkable achievement. A document was placed in the centre column of Belah's eighth pier giving details of the viaduct and ending with this verse:

To further ages these lines will tell
who built this structure o'er the dell –
Wilson with these eighty men
Raised Belah's viaduct o'er the glen.

All that remain today are the buttresses and the pillar supports.

MUSGRAVE

Great Musgrave: 1½ miles south-west of Brough. Little Musgrave: 2 miles south-west of Brough

34
OS Grid Ref: Great Musgrave 766137. Little Musgrave: 760136

Burke's Peerage states that Musgrave was named after a war-like family that lived there for several years. The first Musgrave to be associated with the place was Peter, who lived there about the time of King Stephen, *c.* 1150. Thomas de Musgrave purchased Harcla (Hartley) Castle and added a stone tower to crenelate the buildings, using materials from his Musgrave home, which he abandoned. The two villages, Great and Little Musgrave, were separate townships before 1894, when, under the provisions of the Local Government Act, they were united to form one parish called Musgrave.

35
OS Grid Ref:
767134: Musgrave church.
745157: Warcop church

RUSHBEARINGS

Musgrave and Warcop churches

While the custom of renewing the rushes that covered the clay floors of churches for the most part died out years ago, it is still commemorated in a few English parishes, including three in the old county of Westmorland. Two of these are in the adjoining Eden Valley parishes of Warcop and Musgrave. The Warcop rushbearing takes place on 29 June, St Peter's Day, and at Musgrave about a week earlier. In both parishes girls march behind the band in procession through the village towards the church. They each carry a crown made of flowers and are known as crown bearers. The boys march behind them, carrying rush crosses. During the church service the girls offer their crowns to the vicar, who places them either side of the altar.

BISHOP PERCIVAL

36
OS Grid
Ref: 794125

Near the Black Bull, Brough Sowerby, 1 mile south of Brough

The future bishop destined to become one of the country's foremost educationalists was born in a squat, stone house near the Black Bull, Brough Sowerby. One day, when the boy was about 12 years old, his father was questioned about his future.

'Send t' lad to Appleby Grammar,' the father was advised.

'That's all verra well,' the boy's father hedged. 'But I'm not sure I can afford it.'

'Afford it! By Gow! T' lad's got brains. Thou mun give him a chance to use them.'

The lad's father thought for a moment before replying. Then he said,

'We'll see. I've got some potatoes to sell at Kirkby tomorrow. Trade's been bad lately, but if I get a good price for them, t' lad'll go to Appleby Grammar.'

Next day the potatoes were sold at Kirkby Stephen for a price far in excess of the boy's father's wildest dreams. So, true to his word, he sent his son to Appleby Grammar where the boy excelled, going on to become Bishop Percival, the celebrated head of Rugby School.

37
OS Grid
Ref: 790145

BROUGH CASTLE

Church Brough south of the A66 Brough bypass

In 1092 King William Rufus began building a castle at Brough on the site of the Roman fort of Verterae, a hilltop above Swindale Beck. Its keep, known as the Roman Tower, dates from the latter part of the twelfth century. Brough Castle was involved in the Plantagenet wars against Scotland; and in June 1300 Edward I, 'Hammer of the Scots', stayed there on his way to lay siege to Caelaverock Castle, near Dumfries. On 6 September 1307 Edward III stayed at Brough Castle with the corpse of his father. In 1325 Edward II was again at Brough Castle. In 1521 the castle was destroyed by fire, and remained in ruins until Lady Anne Clifford largely rebuilt it. Much of the old castle was demolished in 1714, many materials and fittings being used to repair Appleby Castle. Much of the stone was used to build houses and barns at Brough.

FOX TOWER

North of the A66 (T) I mile S.W. of Brough

38
OS Grid
Ref: 785164

Halfway up the steep western escarpment of the Pennines in Helbeck Wood, about a mile north-west of Brough, two cylindrical stone towers, one much wider than the other, stand side by side in magnificent isolation on an eminence close to a tarn. This is Fox Tower, built in 1775 by John Metcalf Carleton of nearby Helbeck Hall. From it there is a superb view of the Eden Valley and the fells beyond. Legend has it that Metcalf Carleton had it built as a vantage point for observing foxes, hence its name. However, during the eighteenth century the building of gazebos was something of a status symbol, and it is more likely that John Metcalf Carleton built Fox Tower as a gazebo or belvedere.

Until the Second World War the path climbing between trees to Fox Tower was a favourite walk for locals. But as the war got into its stride, an army camp was built at Warcop and a large area of the Pennines between Brough and Hilton, to westwards, was commandeered as an Armoured Fighting Vehicles range, which it remains to this day. This effectively placed Fox Tower out of bounds for the general public.

39
OS Grid
Ref: 755203

ROMAN FELL

North of A66 between Brough and Warcop

Despite its name, Roman Fell, that clearly defined part of the Pennines' steep, western scarp that lies between Brough and Warcop, has no connection with Rome. It was originally called Rutman Fell, but down the centuries this became corrupted to Roman Fell. Today the whole of Roman Fell has been incorporated into Warcop's RAC Range. This puts it out of bounds to the general public. However, although Roman Fell is strictly off limits, the A66 runs close to it, so its natural beauty can still be appreciated, even at a distance. Army personnel who use Roman Fell as a training area for Army Fighting Vehicles (AFV) live in a permanent camp between Warcop and the A65.

THE HELM WIND

Along the Pennines' western scarp west of Brough

40
OS Grid Ref: Between 525616 and 795145

The only wind in Britain to be given a name is the Helm Wind, which is confined to that part of the Pennines between Brampton in Gilsland and Brough. When the Helm is 'on', its presence can be seen as well as felt. First, a long, thick, white cloud, the Helm Cloud, forms along the top of the Pennines, while simultaneously another parallel line of cloud, dark and swirling, forms an almost stationary band between 3 and 4 miles from the foot of the Pennines. This is called the Helm Bar. Between these two banks of cloud the Helm Wind blows with such fury that it roars down the Pennines' scarp in a bitterly cold blast that suddenly ceases when under the Helm Bar. Since the Helm Bar forms above the River Eden the Helm Wind never crosses the river. The Helm Wind is very destructive, especially in springtime, when it withers vegetables. Once 'on', the Helm Wind can blow for hours, destroying plant life, stripping leaves from trees, causing grazing animals to shiver and sometimes driving them headlong before it. The wind is only of benefit to farmers when it blows during a wet haytime. It can last for days at a time and stops as suddenly as it starts.

41
OS Grid
Ref: 765153

BROUGH HILL FAIR

Brough Hill, east of Brough

Brough Hill Fair, one of the oldest fairs in England, was established at Brough by charter from Edward III to Roger de Clifford. It was originally a four-day event, two days preceding the feast of St Matthew, the day of the fair itself (21 September) and the following day. At some unspecified date the fair became a two-day event, held on 30 September and 1 October. Now it lasts only one day, 30 September. The fair moved to its present site at Brough Hill, 2 miles from Brough, in Warcop parish in about 1661 because of the prevalence of plague at Brough. Until 1800 the fair was extensive but today people are attracted to it mostly to see the gypsies and renew old friendships. The fair has long been associated with bad weather and this has given rise to the term 'Brough Hill weather'.

WARCOP

42
OS Grid
Ref: 746155

Warcop is 3 miles west of Brough

Every springtime Warcop, one of the loveliest villages in the Eden Valley, is smothered in the blossom of the cherry trees that grow profusely in Warcop Hall Park. A clear, gurgling stream flows through the middle of the village, running under a hump-backed bridge and passing close to the village green with its tall maypole before reaching the nearby River Eden. Many ducks occupy this beautiful beck, feeding as fancy takes them. The village once had a castle named after the de Warcops, and today the road from the village centre towards Warcop station is called Castle Hill. Some of the castle's building materials were used in the construction of Kirkby Stephen parish church tower.

43
OS Grid
Ref: 748155

BARON GLENAMORA

Warcop, south of A66, 3 miles north-west of Brough

Edward Short was born at Warcop on 17 December 1912. His teaching career was interrupted by the Second World War, when he served as a captain in the Durham Light Infantry. Afterwards, he returned to teaching and in 1947 became Head of the Princess Louise County Secondary School, Blythe, a position he held until 1951, when he entered Parliament as MP for Newcastle Central. Between 1964 and 1966 he was Chief Whip and Secretary to the Treasury. Between 1968 and 1970 he was Secretary of State for Education and Sciences. In 1972 he became Deputy Leader of the Labour Party, resigning in 1976 to become Chairman of Cable and Wireless. In 1977 he was made a life peer with the title Baron Glenamora, a creditable achievement by any standards.

SANDFORD 'ON THE MIRE'

44
OS Grid
Ref: 729162

4 miles south-east of Appleby-in-Westmorland

Robert de Sandford's son William became the first recorded owner of the Manor of Sandford. It was he who gave Sandford Wood and all the turbary of the township to Robert de Veteripont in return for his discharge from homage and service, ten marks of silver and one palfrey. Later, the same Robert de Veteripont gave it back to William's son, Robert de Sandford, for £20. The Sandfords kept it for several generations, but in time all the heirs were daughters who, through marriage, passed Sandford on to the Berdesey and Warcop families. Until the Second World War, when much of the surrounding marsh was drained to increase food production, Sandford was known locally as Sandford 'on the mire'.

45
OS Grid
Ref: 650132

GAYTHORNE HALL

Gaythorne Hall, 2 miles west of Great Asby

Situated west of Great Asby, alongside Scale Beck, Gaythorne Hall was built in the late sixteenth century and altered during the eighteenth century. It is a home with a grim tale to tell. At one time a married couple, a Protestant husband and his Catholic wife, lived there. When their son was born they began to quarrel over which faith the child should follow. Failing to reach an agreement, they decided to teach him no religion at all. In fact, they decided to teach him nothing at all. The boy was forced to live in a cellar like an animal, was fed on pigswill and given no proper clothes. Before long the child began to look and act like a beast. Six years after his confinement some builders, carrying out repairs to Gaythorne Hall, heard yells coming from the cellar and, on investigation, found a hideous, lice-infested creature with nails like claws. The boy was rescued and his parents prosecuted. The boy grew up to be a respectable young man and held a responsible position, living to a great age. It is more likely that the story was invented to stir up religious prejudice, which was prevalent at the time.

RUTTER FALLS

46
OS Grid Ref: 682158

3 miles south of Appleby-in-Westmorland

Dry Beck has its source on lonely Maulds Meaburn Moor, some 6 miles south of Appleby-in-Westmorland, while Scale Beck begins a little further south, on Bank Moor. For almost 3miles these two streams retain their separate identities, then merge to become Hoff Beck, which meanders northwards to join the Eden near Colby. A mile down stream of where Dry Beck and Scale Beck meet, this lively stream plunges over Rutter Falls, a sheer drop of about 20ft, which, when in spate, is most impressive.

47
OS Grid
Ref: 708167

NOTABLE TREES

Road junction at Little Ormside

In 1333 Edward Balliol, King of Scotland, visited Robert de Clifford at Brougham Castle where, it is said, 'they ran a stag by a single greyhound called, Hercules out of Whinfell Park' to Ninekirks and back, where both died as they 'leaped over the poles'. The stag's horns were nailed to a nearby tree and this rhyme records what happened:

Hercules kills Hart-a-geese
And Hart-a-geese killed Hercules.

The stag's horns gradually became embedded in the tree, which became known as Hart's Horn Tree.

The Three Brothers were three very tall oak trees in Whinfel Park. One measured 18yd in circumference. All have now perished.

The Cedar of Lebanon at Little Ormside (below)was brought from the Middle East in the rim of a sailor's hat, where it was watered regularly. It was planted where it now stands, to become the tall tree it is today.

GREAT ORMSIDE

Great Ormside: 2½ miles south-east of Appleby-in-Westmorland

48
OS Grid
Ref: 702173

One of Great Ormside's claims to fame is that it was one of the least important stations on the Settle–Carlisle line and never generated much traffic. Great Ormside – 'Orm's hill or headland' – is named after Orm, the Viking governor of Appleby Castle. The church is dedicated to St James. Situated on a hill close to the Eden, it is reached through a farmyard, formerly part of Ormside Hall. The building is now a scheduled monument, having been a burial place for 2,000 years. It has a square base to its gabled roof but has neither tower nor spire nor any stained glass. However, it does have a leper's squint, and an Ormside priest called John is said to have drawn up the will of the Black Prince. In 1823 the ninth-century gold and silver 'Ormside Cup' was found in Ormside churchyard. In 1899 a hoard of Viking weapons was found at Great Ormside.

49
OS Grid
Ref: 604109

BLACK DUB MONUMENT

3 miles south-south-west of Crosby Ravensworth

On 8 August 1651 Lady Anne Clifford wrote in her diary: 'His Most Gracious Majesty, King Charles II, with his army, on his way from Scotland, passing Appleby about seven miles to the west.' The King rested his army on Crosby Fell near the source of the River Lyvennet, 2,786ft above sea level. Here a local shepherd, Thwaytes, acted as a guide, leading the army over the moors. In 1843 a freestone obelisk was erected to commemorate the event. The inscription says: 'Here at Black Dub, the Source of the Lyvennet, Charles II Regaled His Army On Their March From Scotland, August 8th, 1651.'

BRACKENBER MOOR GHOSTS

Brackenber Golf Course, east of Appleby-in-Westmorland, north of A66

Appleby Golf Course is sited about a mile east of Appleby-in-Westmorland, between Coupland and Hilton. It occupies part of Brackenber Moor where, long ago, two brothers quarrelled so fiercely that one died of his injuries. Soon after this sad affair local people reported hearing strange sounds; and it did not take long for Brackenber Moor to gain the reputation for being haunted. In 1832 George Pearson of Brough composed a poem of sixteen stanzas telling of the ghostly happenings on Brackenber, the first of which reads:

> 'Twas on a wild and dreary night,
> As o'er bleak Brackenber I hied;
> No friendly planet lent it light
> The wand'rer's lonely steps to guide.

This poem had the salutary effect of exorcising the Brackenber Moor Ghosts.

51
OS Grid
Ref: 605176

REAGILL GRANGE'S HAUNTED GATE

Reagill Grange, a good mile west of Meaburn Hall

The Lyvennet, one of the Eden's most pulchritudinous feeders, has its share of ghosts. Just over a mile west of Meaburn Hall, itself north of Maulds Meaburn at Reagill Grange, there is a gate which, as you approach it at night, will open silently before you and, as silently, close behind you. At several places in the vicinity a figure is apt to suddenly appear in front of you, pass by and, just as suddenly, vanish. At other times an animal – a dog, a calf or a pig – will present itself and quickly grow to three or four times its usual size, which can be disconcerting!

Chapter 2

The Lower Eden Valley

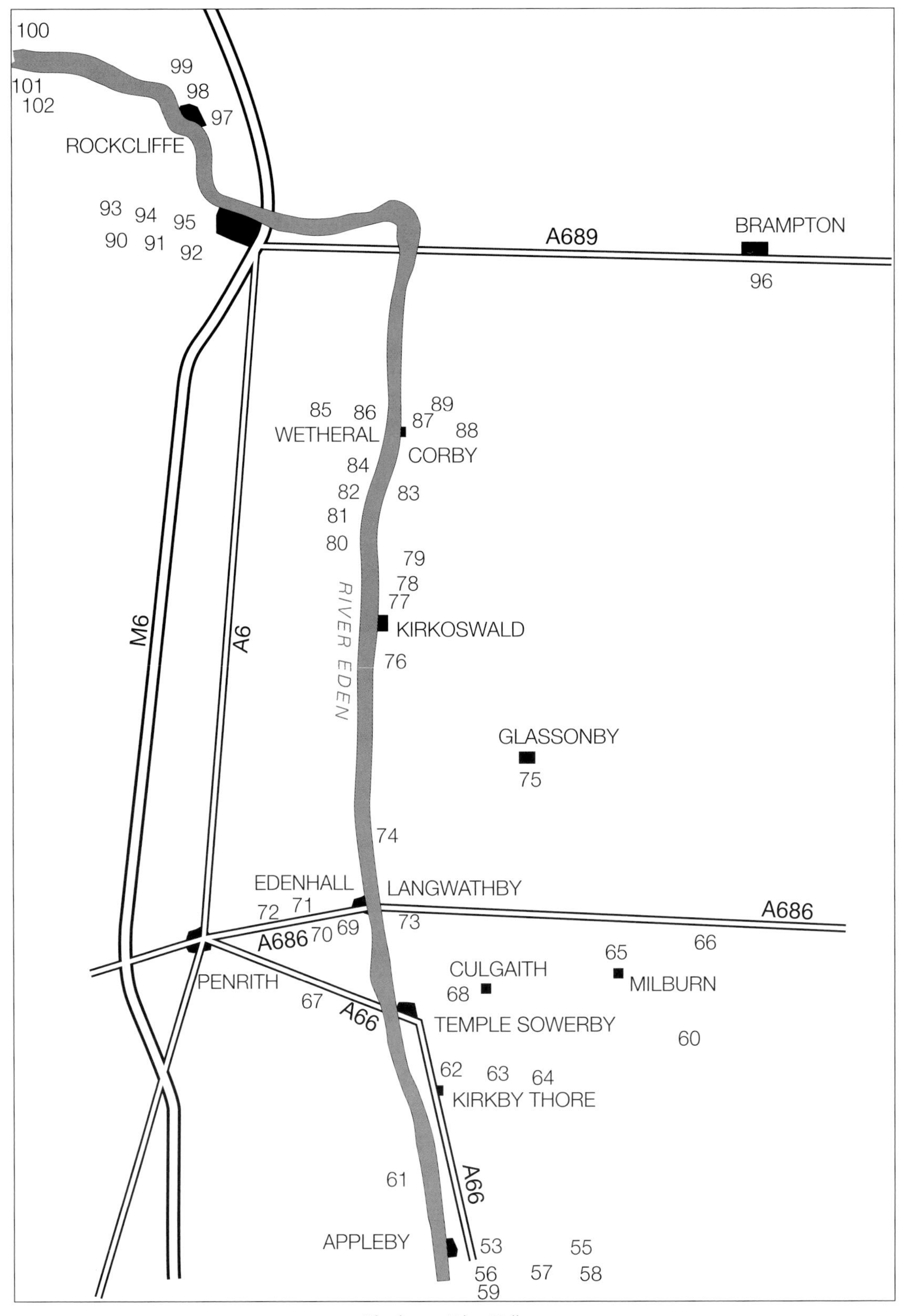

The lower Eden Valley.

APPLEBY CASTLE

52
OS Grid
Ref: 685201

The south end of Boroughgate, Appleby-in-Westmorland

Ranulph de Meschines built Appleby's first castle, a motte and bailey type, which in 1174 was captured and partly destroyed by William the Lion of Scotland. Following a siege, the castle was again taken by Cromwell's army and suffered considerable damage. This was repaired by Lady Anne Clifford, Countess of Pembroke, whose castle it was. Lady Anne defied Cromwell, remaining a staunch Royalist, and was overjoyed when Charles II was restored to the throne. The existing castle was added to and its front rebuilt in the seventeenth century. The Norman keep and two ancient towers remain, all in an excellent state of preservation. The deep moat surrounding the castle is one of the finest earthworks in the country.

53
OS Grid Ref:
Low Cross:
684202.
High Cross:
685201

APPLEBY'S HIGH AND LOW CROSSES

Boroughgate, Appleby-in-Westmorland

When, in 1777, Nicholson and Burn wrote what still remains the standard authority on local history and antiquities, they described Appleby as thus:

> a handsome small town containing between 70 and 80 families consisting principally of one broad street terminated on the north by the church and rising by an easy ascent to the castle on the south, with two handsome crosses or obelisks, one at each end.
>
> Into the upper cross is inscribed the Clifford motto:
>
> Retain your loyalty
> Preserve your rights.
>
> The shambles and town hall in the middle of this street greatly incommode it. If these were taken away, and removed to more proper places, the street, from its natural situation and openness would be very grand and elegant.

High Cross, the cross nearer the castle, was built in the eighteenth century. Low Cross is also eighteenth century, but much later than High Cross. The Clifford motto was added to High Cross at a later date by John Robinson (1772–1802), twice Member of Parliament for Westmorland and six times, until his death, Member for Harwich.

The crosses replaced 'two stately scaffolds' that had been erected at each end of Appleby to celebrate the Restoration of the monarchy in 1660. They were pressed into use on other occasions as well: in April 1856, for example, when Elizabeth Jackson of Kirkby Thore was found guilty of stealing money to the value of one shilling, she was gaoled 'until Saturday next and then to be stripped from the waist upwards and be publicly whipped during the time of the market from the High Cross, Appleby, back to the gaol and that from hence forth she be discharged upon payment of Fees'.

55
OS Grid
Ref: 685202

LADY ANNE'S ALMSHOUSES

Boroughgate, Appleby-in-Westmorland

On 31 December 1650 Lady Anne Clifford purchased some land for £36 on the east side of Boroughgate, Appleby-in-Westmorland, near Appleby Castle, on which she built some almshouses. The foundation stone was laid on 23 April 1652 and the first inmates were admitted the following January and February. To qualify they had to be 'poor and decrepit women inhabiting the dwelling there [Appleby parish], and in the neighbouring parts who, on account of their great old age and great debility of body, are not able to gain their food and clothing by labor'. One of the eleven rules drawn up by Lady Anne was that 'the mother and sisters do all of them endeavour to live quietlie and peaceably amongst themselves'.

THE HOUSE THAT JACK BUILT

56
OS Grid
Ref: 684203

Bondgate, Appleby-in-Westmorland

John Robinson, the son of an Appleby shopkeeper, was educated at Appleby Grammar School then apprenticed to an attorney. While still a young man he gained employment with Sir James Lowther, 1st Earl of Lonsdale, who soon discovered Robinson's unusual aptitude for mathematics. Under Sir James's patronage John Robinson's rise was meteoric. He became MP for Westmorland and rose through various offices to become Surveyor-General of His Majesty's Woods and Forests, and even became a great friend of King George III. It was when he became MP for Westmorland in 1765 that 'Jack' Robinson rebuilt the house that will always be associated with him. For it was there, in what came to be known as 'the house that Jack built', that he lavishly entertained his many friends, including Lord North, the Prime Minister.

57
OS Grid
Ref: 684204

LADY ANNE CLIFFORD'S TOMB

St Laurence's Church, Appleby-in-Westmorland

Lady Anne Clifford, hereditary High Sheriffess of the County of Westmorland and Lady of the Honour of Skipton-in-Craven, was born at Skipton Castle on 30 January 1590, the third and only surviving child of George Clifford, 3rd Earl of Cumberland and his talented wife, Margaret, daughter of Francis Russell, 2nd Earl of Bedford.

When she was 63 years old Lady Anne recalled, 'I was very happy in my first institution, both in my mynd and bodye.' Her eyes were black and her hair thick and brown, long enough to reach her calf, with a peak of hair on her forehead. Her chin was dimpled like that of her father and her face round like her mother's. Although she grew no taller than 4ft 10in, lack of stature never bothered her and she was proud to have 'an exquisite shape of bodie, resembling my father'. Her memory was excellent, her imagination particularly strong, she had sound judgement and 'a discerning spirit'.

Lady Anne was brought up mainly by her mother, mostly in London, being educated by tutors as was customary with the children of nobility at that time. When 13 years old she began attending Court, where she 'was much beloved by that Renowned Queen Elizabeth'.

Lady Anne's father died in 1605, aged 47, when she was 15. He left her £15,000, a vast sum in those days, but willed his entire estates to his brother Francis, a move that directly opposed an entail made by Edward II to an earlier Clifford, which specified that Clifford lands should always descend to the next heir, irrespective of sex.

Almost immediately after the 3rd Earl's death his wife set about contesting the will on her daughter's behalf. In 1607 mother and daughter travelled north to inspect Lady Anne's rightful inheritance. The stakes were high because the Clifford estates covered most of the old County of Westmorland and the area of Craven in North Yorkshire, altogether about 90,000 acres. They included the castles of Brougham, Appleby, Brough, Pendragon and Skipton.

On 25 February 1609, when Anne was 19, she married Richard Sackville, the Lord Buckhurst, who turned out to be 'a man of spirit and talent, but a licentious spendthrift'. On 2 July 1614 their first child, Lady Margaret, was born at Dorset House. The Sackvilles had four more children, three sons, all of whom died in infancy, and another daughter, Lady Isabella, who married James, the 3rd Earl of Northampton. But the Sackville marriage was not a happy one, and by 1626 it had deteriorated to the point where Lady Anne resolved to return to her family at Brougham Castle. She eventually remarried, becoming in 1630 the second wife of Philip Herbert, the 4th Earl of Pembroke and Mongomery, Lord Chamberlain of the Royal

Household and Knight of the Garter. Lady Anne died on 22 March 1678, aged 86.

She now lies lies in her tomb in the north chapel of St Laurence's Church, Appleby-in-Westmorland. She prepared the tomb in 1655, twenty years before her death in 1675. It displays no fewer than twenty-four shields emblazoned in colours on an upright slab of black marble, fixed to the wall and resting on the tomb and records that main descent of the Cliffords from the time of King John. At one time many people thought that the tomb was in fact a cenotaph, because Lady Anne was not buried there. To settle any doubts the tomb was opened to reveal 'the corpse, not interred orin any coffin but lying in a close fitting leaden shroud on a rough, stone trestle or bench about three feet from the ground immediately under the elaborate monument on the north wall of the church which, it was always said, was erected in her lifetime'. The dimensions of the leaden shroud, which exactly fits the figure, are given as just about 4ft 10in, 'which proves how small she was'. The tomb is now completely sealed.

58
OS Grid
Ref: 681210

APPLEBY GRAMMAR SCHOOL

Slightly north of Battlebarrow Hill, Appleby-in-Westmorland

Appleby Grammar School was founded in the mid-fifteenth century on the west side of School House Lane, now Low Wiend, adjoining St Lawrence's Church. The School's first recorded headmaster was Thomas Whinfell (1487). In 1574 Queen Elizabeth I granted the school a charter.

After centuries of use the school buildings were condemned. They were replaced by the present school buildings, built in 1887. Appleby Grammar School has a flourishing record. Its 'old boys' include six Provosts of Queens College, Oxford, and a great many Fellows and graduates. Portraits of three bishops hang in the school hall; and the list of famous men educated at the school is far too long for inclusion here. Appleby Grammar School is now co-educational.

APPLEBY FAIR

The northern edge of Appleby-in-Westmorland

59
OS Grid
Ref: 681214

Appleby Fair is one of the two largest gypsy fairs in the North of England, the other being Brough Hill Fair. Appleby Fair has existed since 1685, protected by a charter granted by James II. From about 1750 the fair was renamed Appleby New Fair and its date moved forward by one week. Originally the fair lasted for a fortnight, but it is now confined to the second week of June. During the Wednesday of that week a meeting of gypsy elders is held to discuss gypsy welfare. Appleby Fair is renowned for its horse trading, mainly between gypsies and non-gypsy 'travellers'. Before the dealing the horses put up for sale are washed with soap powder in the River Eden. This makes their coats shine but also does nothing for the fish. A few horse drawn vardos still visit Appleby Fair but most of the caravans are modern and vehicle pulled. Their owners vie with each other for the finest displays of fine china and cut glass.

60
OS Grid
Ref: 746263

HIGH CUP NICK

5 miles north-east of Appleby-in-Westmorland

High Cup Gill is a 2-mile long rocky gorge that cuts deep into the heart of the Pennines. The entrance is via Harbour Flat, a farm at the foot of Murton Pike, between Murton and Dufton, 2 miles away. High Cup Gill is made of whinstone, a dark, igneous rock, and it ends at a cleft in a horse-shoe precipice down which High Cup Beck plunges. It is this cleft, not the gorge, that consitutes High Cup Nick. It is guarded by three outliers, Knock Pike (1,306ft), Dufton Pike (1,578ft) and Murton Pike (1,949ft), the result of a whole series of fractures along the Pennine Fault. Collectively, the pikes are called the Cross Fell outliers. 'Pike' is derived from the Old English '*pic*', meaning 'pointed hill'. Near High Cup Nick there is a free-standing basalt column called Nichol's chair or the Nichol chair. It was named after a Dufton cobbler who climbed it, taking with him a pair of boots which he soled and heeled while sitting on the top.

From Nichol's chair, looking almost directly across High Cup Gill, there is a deep cleft in the escarpment down which High Cup Beck falls. This is the real High Cup Nick.

On one memorable occasion a few of us on a cross Pennine walk followed a westwards route which took us along the higher reaches of the River Tees along the foot of Falcon Clints, up the side of Cauldron Snout, a spectacular cataract of foaming spume, past two adjacent farms, Birkdale, the loneliest inhabited place in the old county of Westmorland, across featureless moorland and along infant Maize Beck, which was crossed on a footbridge where it flowed through a limestone gorge. From that footbridge we followed a clear path that led directly to High Cup Gill and a different world. All the wild bleakness of the High Pennines was left behind while ahead and below the calm of the Eden Valley beckoned. It was as though we had gone through a door, exchanging a dull room for one filled with sunshine. It was a scene filled with wonder and it spilled into our lives and enriched them.

61
OS Grid
Ref: 640236

ALL SAINTS', BOLTON

The north side of Bolton, 3 miles north-west of Appleby-in-Westmorland

Do not let the skull and crossbones of a headstone in All Saints' churchyard put you off; picturesque Bolton is a friendly place. Six-petalled rosettes and figured capitals decorate the doorway of the Norman church. On the right, just inside All Saints', there is a poor box dated 1634, while, on the left, the front cover is dated 1687. One of the north windows was originally a Norman doorway, above which is a slab with a carving of two knights jousting. The chancel arch has a fine, carved screen. Throughout this delightful church there is an ambience of peace and contentment.

KIRKBY THORE

4 miles north-west of Appleby-in-Westmorland

62
OS Grid
Ref: 639257

The Roman camp of Bravoniacum was situated near the confluence of Trout Beck and the Eden, close to where Maiden Way branched from the Roman road from York to Carlisle. Today the village is called Kirkby Thore – the name is derived from the Norse 'Thor' and the Hiberno-Celtic 'tuchar', meaning 'highway'. So it is the Roman road that gave Kirkby Thore its name!

A knight called Whelp was the first recorded lord of the manor of Kirkby Thore, during the reign of King Stephen. The church, dedicated to St Michael, has a claim to fame: the bell was cast in York in 1450 and is probably the largest in what was Westmorland. In 1829 a Wesleyan chapel was built in Kirkby Thore.

63
OS Grid
Ref: 612271

LYING COMPETITIONS

Temple Sowerby village green

Temple Sowerby, 'Queen of Westmorland and villages' was the location of an annual lying competition, held on the first day of May. Participants would assemble on the village green to nominate a certain number of candidates who would compete for various prizes. The first prize was a grindstone, the second was a razor-sharpening hone, the third an inferior-quality whetstone, which was given to all those who only attained mediocrity status in the noble art of lying. Each participant began a story and the more improbable it became the greater his chance of success. The people listening to these tales were the judges and awarded prizes for the most deserving. Then they all adjourned to the inns to cap the wild stories with a few jars.

ACORN BANK

1 mile north of Temple Sowerby

64
OS Grid Ref: 618282

Acorn Bank was first occupied by the Knights Templar in the twelfth century. In 1323 the Knights Hospitalers acquired the site. In 1543 Henry VIII granted the manor of Temple Sowerby to the Dalston family, who lived at Acorn Bank for many years until the Boazmans, from County Durham, became owners through marriage. In 1930 Kenneth Boazman sold Acorn Bank, the mill and 120 acres of land to Captain and Mrs McGregor Phillips. Mrs Phillips was the well-known author Dorothy Una Ratcliffe, who wrote many of her books at Acorn Bank. She started a wild flower garden and bird reserve behind the manor, which became a winter sanctuary for wild duck. Badgers and otters lived there, among sixty-five different varieties of daffodils, including Wordsworth's small and wild Lenton Lily, which she introduced. Princess Margaret often stayed at Acorn Bank, which she regarded as a refuge from the pomp of Court life. In 1950 Una Ratcliffe presented Acorn Bank to the National Trust. In 1976 the Sue Ryder Foundation became the tenant of Acorn Bank and converted it into a Sue Ryder home. The garden, run by the National Trust, has one of the most extensive herb gardens in the country.

65
OS Grid
Ref: 655292

MILBURN

3 miles north-east of Temple Sowerby

Milburn is the most northerly village in what was the old county of Westmorland. It was specially built so that it could be easily defended from raiding Scots. It has an oblong village green almost entirely surrounded by houses. In its early days the inhabitants used to close all the entrances to the village, and, during the winter months, turned their cattle on to the green. Milburn's church, dedicated to St Cuthbert, is a quarter of a mile outside the village to the south-west. About ½ mile south-east of the village, on the fellside, is Howgill Castle, the medieval seat of the lords of Milburn Manor. It has been considerably altered but some of the ancient 10½ft thick walls remain. Archery was practised on the village green in days of yore.

CROSS FELL

4 miles north-east of Blencarn

66
OS Grid Ref: 687344

The steep, western scarp of the High Pennines is also the eastern side of the Eden Valley, and the highest part of the Pennines is a plateau, Cross Fell, which is covered with rock and short grass. Near Cross Fell's south-western edge a trig point marks the highest point in the Pennines, 2,930ft above sea level. Slightly north-east of the trig point is a very useful windbreak shaped like a cross. Cross Fell was originally called 'Fiends Fell', a much more appropriate appellation as the landscape may be post-glacial, and is covered in snow and cloud for much of the year. Only mountain birds like the curlew, eagle and dotterel are at home here; to fell walkers, Cross Fell is a challenge. But there is an enigmatic beauty about the ungodly plateau of Cross Fell that makes it unforgettable.

67
OS Grid
Ref: 547290

THE COUNTESS'S PILLAR

South side of the A66, 2½ miles east of Penrith

It was a problem as old as the hills, and Lady Anne dealt with it in the time-honoured way: she went home to mother. Her marriage to Richard Sackville, the Lord Buckhurst, had come to the point of no return and so, on 21 February 1616, she headed north to spend Easter with her mother at Brougham Castle.

Her husband accompanied her to within a mile of Croxhall, where he parted company and returned in his coach to Lichfield, while she continued, in her coach, accompanied by ten retainers and stewards and, ominously, thirteen horses. Derby was her first stop and she arrived there with a heavy heart. She hoped that she and her entourage would all stay at Brougham Castle for Easter, which was early that year, Easter Day being 31 March; and, in fact, that is exactly what happened.

On Easter Monday an order was received from Lady Anne's husband that his coach and all her retinue and horses return to London at once. With great reluctance, Lady Anne complied, having first had a paper drawn up showing that this move was against her wishes. Once they had set off she changed her mind and sent two messengers after them, entreating them to return to Brougham Castle and remain with her.

On 2 April Lady Anne again changed her mind and decided that perhaps it would be best if she returned to her husband. Her mother accompanied her for the first quarter of a mile where they had a very sorrowful parting. Lady Anne never saw her mother alive again. A 14ft column called the Countess's Pillar marks the spot. It stands on a grassy mound on the south side of the A66 about ¼ mile east of Brougham Castle. The pillar is octagonal with square facings above and a pyramid-shaped cap. There are sun dials on its east, west and south sides. On the north side are two heraldic shields, a skull and cross bones and the date, 1654. A brass tablet on its south side reads:

> This pillar was erected in anno domini January, 1654, by ye right Honable Anne, Countess Dowager of Pembroke etc., daughter and sole heire of ye Right Honoble George, Earl of Cumberland etc., for a memorial of her last parting in this place with her good and pious Mother, ye Right Honoble Margaret, countess Dowager of Cumberland, ye 2nd of April, 1616, in memorial whereof she also left an annuity of four pounds to be distributed to ye poor within this Parish of Brougham every 2nd day of April for ever, upon ye stone table here hard by, Laus Deo.

The Countess Pillar

68
OS Grid
Ref: 610298

CULGAITH

2 miles north of Temple Sowerby

Culgaith straddles a hill called 'T Pea' through which the Settle–Carlisle railway line passes along a tunnel, 600yd long. The village has three claims to fame: 'T Pea' hill, its brass band and Atkinson's sausages, which are no longer made there. All Saints', the village church, was built in 1756 on the site of an older one. All Saints' has no stained glass windows, which is unusual in so old an Anglican place of worship. Culgaith's other place of worship is its Wesleyan chapel. The Black Swan is the village's only pub.

Lakeland's eastern fells, including Saddleback, gladden the eye to westwards while, behind, the Pennines sweep in glorious splendour to the skyline.

EDENHALL AND LADIES WALK

69
OS Grid
Ref: 566324

Across the Eden, one mile south of Langwathby

Edenhall, the most recent mansion built in the hamlet of Edenhall, was an elegant piece of architectural splendour in the Italian style, erected in about 1821 in glorious parkland, enhanced by the meandering Eden, the beautiful fourteenth-century church of St Cuthbert with, beyond, the Pennines at their highest. Two splendid cedars of Lebanon stood watch over a beautiful flower garden. A third tree, a lofty cedar, remains, and is one of the tallest trees in England.

In 1860 work began on a fine circular walk that still maintains a link between Edenhall, and Langwathby. It is 3½ miles long and makes an excellent diversion from the main route. It is as bewitching as its name – Ladies Walk. Edenhall mansion was demolished in 1934.

70
OS Grid
Ref: 566324

THE LUCK OF EDENHALL

Edenhall, 1 mile south of Langwathby

Sometimes legends outlive themselves. Sometimes they become irrelevant, as in the case of 'the luck of Edenhall', about which there are several. The most popular 'luck of Edenhall' legend is about one of the Musgrave servants. One day the servant in question went to St Cuthbert's Well, near Eden Hall, to draw water and surprised some fairies at play. They were dancing in a circle at the centre of which was a goblet, which the servant seized. As he did so, the horrified fairies cried out: 'If the cup should break or fall, Farewell the luck of Eden Hall.' The servant gave the goblet to his master and told him what the fairies had said. From then on, the Musgraves ensured that the goblet was kept out of harm's way, and since it remained intact the Musgraves flourished.

Whenever Philip, Duke of Wharton, was staying with the Musgraves he was in the habit of tossing the goblet in the air and catching it as it fell. This horrified the Musgraves who knew that he was sceptical about the legend. From Philip's point of view, this was simply an act of devilment. Every time he threw it in the air, he made sure that he would be able to catch it, because he did not wish to upset his hosts. However the Musgraves were not at all happy with his antics because they were the ones affected by the curse should the goblet be broken.

'The luck of Edenhall' is a tall, green, glass vessel that widens in a gentle curve to end in a graceful lip with geometrical design on it in crimson, blue and yellow. It is thought to have been originally designed as a chalice. It is kept in a leather case that carries the monogram IHS on its top. One theory is that it was brought from Palestine by one of the Musgraves during the crusades. The case said to be fifteenth century: the goblet is much older.

Eden Hall was demolished in 1934 and the Musgrave family, which for so long held an important position in Cumberland and Westmorland, has all but vanished, leaving little trace. But 'the luck of Eden Hall' remains, in the Victoria and Albert Museum in London.

71
OS Grid
Ref: 569321

ST CUTHBERT'S CHURCH, EDENHALL

1 mile south of Langwathby, near Edenhall

The beautiful twelfth-century church of St Cuthbert stands in solitary splendour just inside what was Eden Hll's deer park. During the Border raids the church's fifteenth-century tower was a place of refuge. Archery was once practised in the churchyard; the grooves in the stonework at the eastern end of the church were probably made by the archers sharpening their arrows, and yews for making bows were planted in the churchyard, safely out of reach of livestock.

On the tower's western face there are four carved shields showing the arms of the Musgraves, Veteriponts, Stapletons and Hiltons, four important families whose histories are linked to that of Edenhall. St Cuthbert's east window is thought to be Venetian; and a marble slab inside the altar rail is inlaid with two brass plates depicting Sir William Stapleton and his tiny wife. Sir William died in the middle of the fifteenth century.

THE PLAGUE CROSS

1 mile south of Longwathby, near Edenhall

72
OS Grid Ref: 567323

The plague – typhus – struck Edenhall in the late sixteenth century, killing a quarter of the inhabitants. Today the Plague Cross can be seen inside St Cuthbert's churchyard wall, just past where Ladies Walk path divides. The cross stands on the site of a basin in which vinegar was kept: to prevent the plague spreading, victims used to place money in the vinegar to pay for food brought for them from Penrith. Some sufferers lived in shacks around the church. Others, fearful of catching the disease, fled their homes to the nearby fells.

In the 1870s Lady Musgrave ordered the removal of St Cuthbert's churchyard wall and the stones were used to build the retaining wall of Ladies Walk.

73
OS Grid
Ref: 571336

LANGWATHBY

North bank of the Eden, 11 miles north-west of Appleby-in-Westmorland

Langwathby, 'the settlement at the long ford', was bestowed on Henry Fitz Sweyn by Henry I, who soon afterwards changed his mind and decided to keep it as a royal estate. King John also retained the estate, but Henry III gave it to Alexander, King of Scotland, as part of 200 librates of land granted to the Scots in 1237 in return for the release of Cumberland and Westmorland. The estate remained in the hands of the Scottish monarchy until the defection of John Baliol, when it reverted to the English Crown and was granted by Richard II to Ralph Neville, 1st Earl of Westmorland, to be held by him and his male heirs. In 1471 the manor again reverted to the Crown when Edward IV gave it to his brother Richard, Duke of Gloucester, who became Richard III. The estate remained Crown property until 1696, when William III granted it to William Bentinct, 1st Earl of Portland, in whose family it remained until the Duke of Devonshire purchased it in 1787.

LONG MEG AND HER DAUGHTERS

74
OS Grid Ref: 571372

1 mile north-east of Little Salkeld

Long Meg and her daughters, a stone circle within a bank, is a stone henge. Long Meg itself, the outlier to the south-west of the circle, is aligned so that the midwinter sun sets exactly over it. For Neolithic arable farmers and stock breeders looking for signs of the return of warmer weather this was very important, for at the spring and autumn equinoxes the sun rises due east and sets due west. Long Meg stands close to the crest of a ridge beyond which the ground falls away, steeply, to the Eden on its west side. Anyone approaching from that direction can see the top of Long Meg outlined against the sky as far as a mile away, while her daughters are hidden by the curve of the hill. So perhaps Long Meg had a dual function.

75
OS Grid
Ref: 574401

ROMANY'S BIRD TABLE

Old Parks Farm, near Glassonby

To the Revd George Bramwell Evens his beloved Eden became heaven on earth. Evens was a brilliant communicator who, as Romany of the BBC, had the ability to show people the glory of God through the wonder of nature. He was particularly fond of the glorious countryside around Wetheral, which he featured in his famous *Out with Romany* programmes and books. Old Parks Farm, near Glassonby, where he changed his personality with his clothes, became so close to his heart that his ashes were scattered on a hillock overlooking a beautiful, wooded vale. A neat stone bird table set inside protective railings, marks the spot. The inscription reads: 'Sacred to the memory of Rev. Bramwell Evens, Romany of the BBC, whose ashes are scattered here. Born 1884: Died 20th November, 1943. He loved birds and trees and flowers and the wind on the heath'.

KIRKOSWALD CASTLE

East of Kirkoswald

76
OS Grid
Ref: 559410

Kirkoswald Castle was built in about 1200 by Randolph Engayn and was subsequently improved by Sir Hugh de Morville, who added a park on inheriting the castle along with the manor of Kirkoswald and Lazonby through his wife, Helwise de Stuteville. The great hall was ornamented with portraits of the Kings of England from 'Brute' downwards. For a very long time the great hall was one of the finest in the North of England. The Morville family held the castle until it came into the hands of the Multons. Thomas de Multon and John de Castra made considerable additions to it. About the beginning of the sixteenth century its defences were strengthened by a ditch. In later years Kirkoswald Castle along with the manor of Kirkoswald and Lazonby came to the Dacres. It was Lord Dacre who ordered the castle to be dismantled. In 1688 Kirkoswald Castle was 'little more than a bare shell on a heap of stones'.

77
OS Grid
Ref: 537439

NUNNERY HOUSE

Alongside Croglin Water, 1 mile north-west of Kirkoswald

The name 'Nunnery' derives from the Benedictine convent that had its beginnings in Carlisle when St Cuthbert laid the first foundation there and gave the veil to Ermenburga, Queen Dowager of Northumbria as first abbess. In 1089 William Rufus transferred the convent to Armathwaite, then called Heremitethwaite, where it remained for 'some ages' before being re-established where the eighteenth-century Nunnery House stands today, close to the confluence of Croglin Beck and the Eden. The convent was dedicated to Our Saviour and the Blessed Virgin Mary. Nunnery Walks, which starts at Nunnery House, is one of the most beautiful riverside walks in England.

EDEN GORGE CARVINGS

78
OS Grid Ref: 505455

Eden Gorge

Several sculptured heads are shown in relief on a sandstone bluff in the Eden Gorge near Armathwaite. Alongside them, expertly carved in 2in letters, is William Mounsey's exquisite parody of Isaac Walton's *Compleat Angler*. Some of the letters are back to front. The verse reads:

The Fisher's gentle life
Happiest is of any;
Void of pleasure, full of strife
And beloved by many;
Others are but toys
And to be lamented,
Only this a pleasure is.

In Walton's original, the third line reads 'Full of pleasure void of strife'. The version carved on the bluff is pure Mounsey. (See pages 100 and 102 for more about William Mounsey.)

79
OS Grid
Ref: 478525

CORBY'S SALMON COOPS

Slightly upstream of Wetheral

The Eden is one of the top three salmon rivers in England and Wales. For centuries salmon born in the Eden have returned to spawn in the river of their birth. Between 1167 and 1203 Hugh de Morville of Pendragon Castle in the Eden's upper reaches granted the monks of Holm Cultram Abbey permission to net these returning salmon. During the Middle Ages the tenants of the banks of the Eden's estuary were allowed by the Lord of the Manor to fish from a boat for a lump sum; and in the course of time these rights became divided and again subdivided. The numbers of netters increased enormously, which brought confrontation and led to the Eden and its fisheries being the subject of countless law suits and legal bickerings.

In the fourteenth century monks installed salmon coops at Corby. They were built across a narrow channel from the Eden's right bank to a narrow mid-river island. Pools between the coops were swept with nets by the salmon fishers. Those salmon fortunate enough to escape Corby's salmon coops and a miscellany of other net fishers had to contend with a weir further upstream.

By the 1860s salmon poachers abounded and had become bold enough to work in large gangs at night, sweeping the river. They would then return in broad daylight with their nets and the salmon they had caught slung over their shoulders, defying alike the keepers and the police. In 1985 Mr E.P. Ecroyd brought together the owners of the fishery rights in the River Eden and the Eden Owners Association was founded. In 1987 the Association purchased virtually all the netting rights in the lower river, downstream of Carlisle, and was supported by the North West Water Authority, who brought a by-law preventing any other rights from being exercised. This was immediately followed up by the Association joining owners on the Borders Esk and Annan in contributing to the buying out of the stake netting rights on the Scottish shore of the Solway Firth from the mouth of the River Kirtle to Dornock Burn. These purchases allowed thousands more salmon to pass through the Solway and up the Eden.

One of many fishing stories told by Joe Taylor based on his fifty years as a ghillie at Wetheral concerns a salmon that was caught twice. A fisherman caught a salmon but dropped it into deep water. Joe, his ghillie, and his wife returned to the Eden that night and armed with a rod, large hook and a torch, rowed to where the lost salmon was found 10 feet down. Joe brought it to the surface where his wife netted it. They presented it to the fisherman, astonished to see the salmon that had been caught twice.

80
OS Grid
Ref: 467534

CONSTANTINE'S CELLS

Wetheral Woods

Constantine's Cells are gouged from a rocky cliff face some 40ft above the River Eden in Wetheral Woods. When I was trying to find them a local man gave me directions: 'Continue along this climbing woodland path', he informed me, 'and stay on it until you come to another path leading off to the left. It will bring you to Constantine's Cells. You can't miss it. There is a tall tree where the path leads away from the one you are on.' Since we were already surrounded by the trees of Wetheral Wood, the information he had imparted about the tree marking the junction was not as clear as I would have liked. Nevertheless, I thanked my informant and moved on. Sure enough, smack in the middle of Wetheral Wood I came to a junction on the left. It was marked by a tall tree, so I took it. The path soon led to steps cut into a sandstone cliff, which I descended to reach Constantine's Caves or Cells, which date from pre-Roman times. They are named after Constantine, a local saint, thought to have been King of the Britains in the early days of Christianity, who forsook the Crown to become a missionary under St Kentigern. Constantine is an enigmatic figure, sometimes referred to as a sixth-century prince and sometimes as a tenth-century king. His association with the Wetheral caves that carry his name is a slender one.

With the monks of Wetheral Priory we are on much firmer ground. They most certainly used the caves for hiding their valuables, grain and dependants when the pillaging Scots carried out their swift and savage raids.

Constantine's Cells are gouged from a cliff face 40ft above the River Eden. They are comprised of three chambers, each roughly 20ft long by 10ft wide by 9ft high. A passage 3ft wide by 26ft long fronts these chambers. Daylight enters the cells through windows in the outer wall, which also features a fireplace and a chimney. When the cells were built the only way into them was through a door at the end of the passage several feet above a narrow ledge that ran beneath it. Access was difficult, requiring a ladder, which could be lowered and drawn up again when not in use. Overhanging shrubs and other vegetation rendered the entrance almost invisible.

Soft sandstone attracts graffiti and there is much evidence of this in and around Constantine's Cells. The earliest recorded inscription inside the cells reads, 'T. Monte 1573', since when many other people have added their names in and around them. But top marks for skill and originality must go to Major William Henry Mounsey of Rockcliffe. He had a propensity for gouging enigmatic carvings in inaccessible places mostly along the River Eden. One of his many carvings is halfway down the steps to the cells, close to a symmetrical Star of David, also Mounsey's work. It is a work from the songs of Llywarch Hen, a Welsh poet of the early ninth century which, translated, means: 'This leaf which is being persecuted by the wind, let her beware of her fate. She is old though only born this year.' The letters MWH cut vertically alongside this verse are Mounsey's initials in reverse order. There is also a symbol MA which means Scorpio, the Scorpion being one of the signs of the zodiac.

81
OS Grid
Ref: 467535

MOUNSEY WAS HERE

Constantine's Cells, Wetheral Woods

Some 20yd downstream of the inscription described on page 101, a few feet above normal water level, is another of William Mounsey's enigmatic carvings. It reads:

> To meet the Atlantic's boundless time,
> See Old Ituna's waters glide,
> As rolls the river to the sea
> So time unto eternity.
> O.M. Vo AD 1852.
> YESNUOM SUMEILUG

Ituna is the Roman name for the River Eden.

The capital letters below the date spell GULIEMUS MOUNSEY written backwards. Guliemus is the Latinised form of William.

THE ANGRY EDEN

The Eden's eastern bank at Wetheral

82
OS Grid
Ref: 471545

On Christmas Day 1822 John Mason discovered that the Eden, when angry, is a formidable force. He stood outside his riverbank cottage at Wetheral powerless to do anything as swirling flood-water inexorably rose higher than anyone could remember. Inside the cottage, the terrified tenants prayed that the river would stop rising. When their neighbours realised the danger they were in, they came to the rescue and, with great difficulty, managed to get them out through the cottage's small windows. Progress was slow, and to make matters worse, the wife had to be carried out wrapped in a blanket and carrying her new-born baby. Within minutes of the family being pulled clear of their cottage home, the house collapsed and was washed away.

84
OS Grid
Ref: 467542

WETHERAL PRIORY

Wetheral Priory, Wetheral 6 miles east of Carlisle

Wetheral is a beautiful Eden Valley village with an Anglo-Saxon name that means 'the haugh or steep grassy bank where sheep are kept'. Like good wine it has improved with age, but it has always been a lovely spot. In the third century a small community lived here, close to the edge of Inglewood Forest, once the largest hunting preserve in England. The Angles expanding westwards from their Northumbrian kingdom settled there during the seventh century and for most of the tenth and eleventh centuries it was part of the Scottish kingdom of Strathclyde.

When William II, Rufus, succeeded to the throne in 1087 he determined to settle his northern border. To this end he seized the southern part of Cumbria and made the Solway the north-west boundary of his kingdom and gave the lordship of this district to Ranulf de Meschin, one of his most trusted Norman barons, whose headquarters were at Appleby.

Ranulf de Meschin gave the manor of Wetheral to the Benedictine Abbey of St Mary, York, as an endowment. With usual Norman efficiency he chose a superb site for the monastery on a hillside overlooking the Eden. The mother house sent a prior and twelve monks to set up the monastery, which extended from the present gateway to the river's edge. Within the priory walls there was a church, a guest house and a hospital. Local villagers were given employment working the mill-bay and the salmon sluices and tilling the land.

Ranulf de Meschin took good care to ensure that the salmon sluices and the mill-bay were secured for the priory monks by a separate charter. Neither the fish nor the water on either side of the river below the large pool at the bottom of the priory as far as the Monkswath should be disturbed. This was very important because the salmon caught in the coops there made a valuable contribution to the priory's kitchen. The Lord of Crosby to whom the sluices and the fishing had belonged before they became part of the priory's endowment, received every eighth fish taken.

Wetheral Priory was a place of sanctuary, a privilege granted by Henry I in his Charter of Rights, the boundaries marked by six grith crosses. The word 'grith' is Anglo-Saxon and means 'peace'. Sanctuary could be claimed by anyone who had committed murder 'suddenly without enmity' or 'without laying in wait' through fleeing to the Liberty at Wetheral; they could claim grith by ringing the bell in the church and swearing before the bailiff of the Liberty that they would conduct themselves well and faithfully. They could then live in peace within the Liberty but could not go outside the boundary. All that remains of the priory is the gatehouse, which now belongs to the National Trust.

85
OS Grid
Ref: 467547

THE HOWARD CHAPEL, WETHERAL CHURCH

Wetheral

The original Wetheral church, which Ranulf Meschin gave to the abbey of St Mary's at York, probably had only a nave and a chancel, the aisles being added at a later date. The layout of the church, apart from the tower, which was built in 1760, is much as it was in the fourteenth century. Attached to the north side of the chancel is the Howard chapel, built in 1791 above the thirteenth-century mausoleum of the Roman Catholic Howard family of Corby Castle. Twenty-five members of the Howard family are thought to be buried in this vault, first used in 1663 when Mary, second wife of Sir Francis Howard, was laid to rest there. The last person to be consigned to the vault was Philip, the elder son of Henry Howard, in 1882, when it was finally sealed up.

THE HOLLEKENS STATUE

86
OS Grid
Ref: 468547

Wetheral parish church

The Howard chapel in Wetheral church was built to house a beautiful white marble statue, which was a memorial to Maria, wife of Henry Howard, and her baby daughter, both of whom died in November 1789, Maria aged only 22 years. Joseph Hollekens (1732–1823), an English sculptor whose reputation, in particular for lifelike busts', almost equalled that of Reynolds in painting, was commissioned to do the work. Henry Howard paid him £1,500 for the statue, which shows a draped figure, 'Faith', pointing upwards with her right hand while supporting the head of the dying mother with the other. The mother's dead baby is lying across her lap. This fine group is considered to be Hollekens' greatest work. An avaricious man, Hollekens is said to have burst into tears when he heard where his masterpiece was to be placed because, he thought that it would be seen by so few people.

83
OS Grid
Ref: 470535

'ROMANY' OF THE BBC

Near the Eden at Wetheral

The Revd George Bramwell Evens, 'Romany' of the BBC, was born in Hull in 1884, the son of a *gorgio* (non-gypsy) father and a *romanichais* (gypsy) mother. As a young man he entered the Methodist ministry and moved to Carlisle as the minister of a small Methodist church in September 1914. When not busy with chapel matters he spent his time exploring the Eden, which held such enchantment for him, especially the glorious countryside around Wetheral. His constant companions were his wife Eunice, his dog Raq – he had a succession of spaniels, all called Raq – and his horse, which he called Comma because it seldom came to a full stop. When the Revd Bramwell Evens preached, the words came straight from the heart of Romany.

'Thou wilt come to us in a thousand ways. Thou dost speak to some through the loveliness of the world about us – the odour of it, with the budding hedgerows and the songs of birds. By the mistiness of the hills and the glorious skies dost Thou appeal to us. . . .'

CORBY CASTLE

87
OS Grid Ref: 472542

Corby, across the River Eden from Wetheral

The imposing castle of Corby is superbly poised 90ft above the Eden on a site occupied by a castle since at least the twelfth century. Its oldest part is a fourteenth-century pele tower, which was built by the powerful Salkeld family to guard a ford over the river, half a mile downstream of it. In 1611 the Salkelds sold the property to Lord William Howard, third son of the fourth Duke of Norfolk. When the property changed hands only the pele tower was standing. Lord William Howard added a two-storeyed L-shaped house on to the back of it. A finely sculpted lion proudly guards the castle from a rooftop vantage point. Magnificent at any time of the year, the lion is best seen at midnight on New Year's Eve, when, according to legend, it wags its tail.

88
OS Grid
Ref: 472542

'THE RADIANT BOY'

Corby Castle, Great Corby

Lord William Howard of Corby Castle employed two workmen, a blacksmith and his apprentice, during the building of a house on to the back of the pele tower. The apprentice's job was to lead the castle's roof. He had to collect the lead by donkey cart and bring it to the forge to be melted and rushed to the roof, there to be beaten into shape to seal the castle from the weather. One day while he was working on the roof, one of the Howards opened a window below him. Distracted, he fell from the roof into a tray filled with molten lead. It was an accident: no one was to blame. The youth was not killed instantly. Covered in molten lead, he managed to climb out of the tray as the lead ate away at his body. He staggered forward for a few yards before dying on his feet with one arm pointing to the Howard in the open window, the molten lead glowing in the wind, making the youth glow red. The ghost of this youth has haunted Corby Castle regularly since 1611 and the red glow it emits has earned it the name 'the radiant boy'.

WETHERALL VIADUCT

89
OS Grid
Ref: 466547

The Eden at Wetheral

'The banks of the River Eden about Corby are worthy of notice both on account of their natural beauty and the viaduct which have recently been carried over the bed of the river and a neighbouring ravine.' So wrote the discerning William Wordsworth.

Wetherall viaduct, the one over the Eden, was built between 1830 and 1833 to carry the old North Eastern Railway from Carlisle to Newcastle. It is a huge structure, 625ft long and 99ft high with five semi-circular arches, each 80ft wide. It has red sandstone facing, which blends so beautifully with the red sandstone cliffs at either side of the river. The viaduct contains an iron footbridge and the views it commands are magnificent.

When the railway was opened many thought that Sunday rail travel was ungodly. One clergyman, shocked at the prospect, distributed a notice which read:

Reward For Sabbath Breaking.
People taken safely and swiftly to Hell next Lord's Day by the Carlisle Railway for 7/6. It is a pleasure trip.

90
OS Grid
Ref: 400555

CARLISLE'S WEST WALLS

The west side of Carlisle Cathedral

The only surviving remnants of the old city wall, known as the West Walls, are to be found along the west side of Carlisle Cathedral, some distance away from it. In 1978 excavations towards the south end of the West Walls revealed traces of a gate which, when built, was called Newgate. For over 500 years there was little change in Carlisle's population and its citizens were contained within the city walls. At the begining of the nineteenth century this changed. By 1850 the population had exploded beyond the city walls, which had fallen into advanced decay; and with more land being needed for dwellings the city wall was gradually demolished. Today only West Walls remain.

THE SETTLE–CARLISLE RAILWAY

Between Carlisle and Aisgill

91
OS Grid Ref: Carlisle: 406550. Aisgill: 776977

From its northern terminus, Carlisle's Citadel station, England's greatest scenic railway climbs southerly along the Eden Valley, reaching its highest point, Aisgill, at the head of Mallerstang. Known as the long drag, this spectacular line offers breathtaking views all along the Eden Valley, which is dominated by Cross Fell, the highest point in the Pennines. The line was opened in 1876 by the Midland Railway in competition with two established routes to Scotland. Using many dramatic viaducts and tunnels, the line remains in the glorious scenery of Eden Valley and the Yorkshire Dales throughout.

92
OS Grid
Ref: 401559

CARLISLE CATHEDRAL

Near the centre of Carlisle

Carlisle Cathedral is not as large as its southern counterparts, but it is more beautiful than most. Part of its Norman nave remains, having escaped the Victorian passion for 'improving'. The cathedral was founded as an Augustinian priory in 1123 by King Henry I. In 1133 the Diocese of Carlisle was created, and the priory served several purposes. It was a house of Augustinian canons, mother church of the diocese and the parish church of St Mary. Following the Dissolution of the Monasteries in the 1530s the priory at Carlisle survived because it fulfilled a diocesan and a parochial function.

TULLIE HOUSE

93
OS Grid
Ref: 399558

Abbey Street, Carlisle

Thomas Tullie, Dean of Carlisle, built Tullie House in 1689 on the site of Carlisle's Roman forum. When sewers were renewed in Abbey Street, an almost unspoilt Georgian thoroughfare and Roman foundations were found. The 'shrine' in Tullie House gardens may be part of the forum's complex. Tullie House was described by Pevsner as 'the most ambitious house in Carlisle'. It is Carlisle's only Jacobean building and its drainpipes are works of art. In 1893 members of the wealthy textile family, the Ferguson brothers, made a substantial financial contribution towards the £20,000 cost for the conversion of Tullie House into a museum and library.

94
OS Grid
Ref: 395561

CARLISLE'S COUNTY GAOL

Area covered by Burtons and Woolworths, Carlisle

The gaol began as a dungeon in Carlisle Castle during the twelfth century and 200 years later, like the rest of the castle, was in disrepair. The dungeon contained bow seats into which prisoners were chained by the neck to die by strangulation if they fell off. When the outer gateway of the castle was built in 1387 it incorporated the city's first built-in prison. Two hundred years later part of the citadel was converted into the county gaol but, because of impending civil war, another site had to be found for it because the citadel was needed for the city's defence. The new gaol opened in 1824 could accommodate seventy prisoners, but the average prison population was about forty. The gaol was closed in 1922 as part of a government economy measure and demolished in 1932. The following year Burtons and Woolworths opened stores on the site.

CARLISLE CASTLE

North of Carlisle's ring road

95
OS Grid Ref: 396562

Carlisle's Norman motte and bailey castle is magnificent. Its stone keep was built by David I of Scotland in about 1150 and the rest has been rebuilt and reinforced several times during its long and troubled history. Stone walls projecting southwards towards Carlisle's ring road form the city walls, linking the castle to the city in a continuous barrier that made attack difficult. The massive sandstone walls of the outer, south-facing bailey contain de Ireby's Tower, the impressive outer gatehouse which has been the main entrance to the castle from the twelfth century. The keep is behind the walls. To the east is the site of Queen Mary's Tower, where Mary Queen of Scots was incarcerated for a short time in 1568.

96
OS Grid
Ref: 535612

LIZZIE, THE BRAMPTON WITCH

Brampton Church 6 miles north-east of Wetheral

Elizabeth Douglas was born in Castle Douglas in 1729 and moved to Brampton where she eloped with John Baty, a schoolmaster, to a place near Bewcastle, where they made a living by fortune telling. Later they moved to Brampton Fell, where John Baty died. Lizzie had a long life, surrounded by so much mystery that she became known as Lizzie the witch. She never attended church but 'had regard for God's word'. All the many stories about her had a macabre flavour. One of the strangest concerned a young woman whose ambition was to wear a white bridal gown. Telling her fortune, Lizzie told her, 'Thou needent bother the sel about a white dress: thou'll git a white dress sune enough.' No one understood Lizzie's words, but the following Tuesday the young woman caught a chill, which developed into a fatal fever – the white dress was a burial shroud.

Joseph Parker, a friend, supplied Lizzie with groceries. In return she bequeathed him her set of china which had a spell attached to it. Good luck would come to any member of Joseph Parker's family who drank from the cups. But if the china ever left the family disaster would befall the new owner. The china remains in the Parker family's possession.

Lizzie died at the age of 88. Her funeral took place on 6 March 1817 in some of the wildest weather in living memory, with thunder, lightning and strong winds. It was so dark, mourners had to use lanterns at the graveside. The strong wind penetrated the lantern shutters, blowing out the candles, which had to be relit again and again. She is buried beside her husband.

SMUGGLING AT ROCKCLIFFE

97
OS Grid Ref: 357618

Rockcliffe, 4½ miles north-west of Carlisle

During the 1850s smuggling was rife on the Borders, largely because of the different levels of duty in England and Scotland. Whisky and brandy cost five times more in England than in Scotland. Furthermore, the spice of adventure in outwitting the Excise men was an added attraction. Three or four excise men were stationed at Rockcliffe. They watched the road leading from Springfield in Scotland and kept an eye on Rockcliffe Marsh.

A tin canister, shaped like a pair of woman's corsets, was kept in most Rockcliffe houses. They were buckled with a leather strap in front and held a good supply of 'mountain dew'. So in Rockcliffe, where bread was scarce, there was always a good supply of whisky.

98
OS Grid
Ref: 357618

ROCKCLIFFE CASTLE

Rockcliffe, 4½ miles north-west of Carlisle

Rockcliffe Castle was built by the Dacres, Lords of the Barony of Burgh, to defend their territory near Rockcliffe ford; a castle is first mentioned in 1539. A report dated 1583 states that 'Rokele Castle is the furthest strength of the west borders adjoining to Scotland and the sea'. Rockcliffe Castle was an important meeting place for the wardens of the western March. It was also used as a place of confinement for several Scottish prisoners. In 1570, during an abortive rising, Leonard Dacre seized Rockcliffe Castle but was obliged to evacuate it after a few months and flee to Scotland. Lord Hunsdon took possession of the castle in the Queen's name. Following the union of the two Crowns Rockcliffe Castle fell into ruin and was sold in 1692 by Henry Howard, Duke of Norfolk, the then Lord of the Burgh, to the Revd Charles Usher. It was then destroyed and its material used to build a mansion, the Old Hall.

ROCKCLIFFE FERRY

Near Rockcliffe, 3 miles north-west of Carlisle

99
OS Grid Ref: 358614

Although there have been ferrymen and women at Rockcliffe for almost 400 years, the earliest recorded ferryman is Mr Carter, better known as 'Bet o' the boat', who, along with his wife, worked the ferry during the nineteenth century.

When, in 1893, ferryman John Ervine asked the local squire for a new boat, which could be got for £10, the reply was unhelpful: 'Buy one yourself out of the ferry fees.' The ferry fees were then a penny a crossing, a sum that had remained constant for 300 years.

Perhaps the most infamous ferry user was William Joyce, 'Lord Hawhaw', who, in his Second World War anti-British propaganda broadcasts from Germany, which began 'Gairmany calling . . .' singled out 'the little village of Rockcliffe, with its ferry' and mentioned Bella and Jack Edgar, who worked it. Both are now dead. William Joyce was executed in London in 1946 and the ferry no longer operates.

100
OS Grid
Ref: 334626

THE WALLS OF TROY

Solway Marches, near the Eden's mouth

In 1808, the year William Henry Mounsey was born, only one turf maze existed on the Solway Marches. In 1815 Christopher Graham, an apprentice seaman, cut a larger one immediately east of the original. Then Robert Edgar, a sailor, cut a third one, copied from and identical to Graham's maze. These mazes, called 'the walls of Troy', were simply one continuous curve from the centre outwards, with no misleading cul-de-sacs. It was these turf mazes, now lost through time, weather and the ravages of cattle, that stimulated William Mounsey's life-long association with all things stranger and obscure.

HAUNT OF THE WILD GEESE

101
OS Grid
Ref: 330616

The mouth of the River Eden, 5 miles north-west of Carlisle

With every September moon the calls of pink-foots, greylags and barnacle geese fill the Solway sky. For the Solway is a 'clearing house' for thousands of geese, most of which, having rested, move on. The pink-foots go to East Anglia via Stainmore, greylags head for the Kent estuary and the barnacle geese, having wintered on Rockcliffe Marsh, move on to Longtown. Other geese, like the bean, winter on Rockcliffe Marsh, only in smaller numbers. Rockcliffe Marsh, where the rivers Eden and Esk flow into the Solway Firth, comprise an area of about 1,200 flat green acres and has an outline that is never constant because of its ever changing water courses. Over 5,000 geese are seen regularly there every autumn.

102
OS Grid
Ref: 318600

THE SOLWAY SPACEMAN

The Solway Marshes: west of Carlisle

Having spent all its life in one of the most beautiful valleys in the country the River Eden now tidal and flowing wide and deep, expands as though to embrace the Solway Firth, edging Burgh Marsh and merging with the River Esk before being swallowed by the Irish Sea.

Burgh Marsh and Rockcliffe Marsh are part of an Area of Outstanding Natural Beauty, which along with some 40 square miles of the Solway Firth, is an important winter haunt for wildfowl. Wildfowling has been carried on there for centuries, firstly for food but latterly for sport. Shooting permits are limited to prevent too much disturbance to the wild geese on the 'merge' and thanks to this restriction relations between wildfowlers and conservationists are very good.

Edward Longshanks (1239–1307), was one of the most capable of the medieval English kings. Following his invasion of Scotland and the setting up of an English parliament, he became known as 'the Hammer of the Scots'. However, a national rising, led first by William Wallace, then by Robert Bruce, caused him serious setbacks and he realised that a major campaign against the Scots was needed. Edward journeyed north to re-establish his authority in Scotland during the summer of 1306. He was not in a fit state of health for such a campaign but so determined was he that on 3 July of that year he set out from Carlisle. By now he was suffering from dysentery and his progress was hardly 2 miles a day. He spent the night of 6 July 1307 on Burgh Marsh and when, on 7 July 1307, his servants came to lift him from his bed so that he could eat, he died in their arms. He was 68 years old.

A wooden monument was built on the spot, but it rotted – as did a replacement wooden one. Then, early in the eighteenth century, a stone monument was erected there to replace the two wooden ones. It was financed partly by Lord Lonsdale. More recently, when the monument developed a tilt, a local girl informed the Queen, who arranged for it to be straightened. It is now protected by the Crown. So the River Eden retains its historical connections to the very end, as it does so with its natural history connections.

Every year, as regular as clockwork, as sure as the harvest moon rides the autumn sky, the first of the wild geese return to winter on the Solway, a low lying, dangerous area of shifting sands and treacherous, fast moving tides. Solway means 'muddy ford' and in medieval times this route across the Eden to Scotland from Burgh Marsh was in regular use.

On 23 May 1964 James Templeton of Carlisle and his wife Anne, took their younger daughter, Elizabeth, then 5 years old, to Burgh Marshes. It was a lovely day and the sky was blue and cloudless.

While there, James took three photographs of Elizabeth. They were taken within minutes. When James went to collect the prints he was told by the assistant that one had been spoiled.

'How do you mean – spoiled?' James enquired.

The assistant showed him the prints. Two were almost identical, as one would expect them to be; and, in fact the third one was too; but the third picture also included a spaceman looking over her shoulders. It was not a blur: it was as clear as a bell. Moreover, when James had taken the photos, the sky had been clear; there had been no sight of any other figures in the area apart from Elizabeth and there was no other explanation for the figure on the third photo. Carlisle police were informed and both films and camera were sent to the police laboratories at Preston where the police experts were baffled. The film was sent to Kodak, who, also, could not explain the spaceman. They confirmed that it was not a double exposure. UFO experts were shown the print and they confirmed that it was genuine. There was no trace of any reflections or of anything else that could have interfered with the picture. This extraordinary story was featured in UFO magazines and on nationwide TV but has never been satisfactorily explained.

It would appear that the charm of the Eden Valley is not confined to earthly standards. It seems that people from outer space have also been alerted by its beauty. So, when people talk of the Eden Valley being a heaven on earth they are pretty close to the truth. It is a lovely thought. Meanwhile, the Solway spaceman remains an enigma.

Above: The Solway spaceman?
Right: Monument marking the site where 'the Hammer of the Scots' died on Solway Marshes.

FURTHER READING

F.B. Chancellor, *Around Eden*, J. Whitehead and Son (Appleby) Ltd, 1954.
Charlie Emett, *In Search of Westmorland*, Cicerone Press, 1985.
——, *The Eden Way*, Cicerone Press, 1990.
——, *Eden Tapestry*, Cicerone Press, 1995.
——, *The Walker's Guide to the Eden Valley*, Smith Settle, 1999.
Neil Hanson, *Walking Through Eden*, Futura Publications, 1990.
Martin W. Holdgate, *Historic Appleby*, J. Whitehead and Son (Appleby) Ltd., 1956.
Mike McCarthy, *Carlisle*, Sutton Publishing, 1993.
R.R. Sowerby, *Historic Kirkby Stephen and North Westmorland*, Titus Wilson and Son Ltd, 1950.

INDEX

Natural Features

People

Roads and Railways

Songs

Supernatural

Traditions and Customs

Villages

Wildlife